Words of Life

Words of Life

JESUS AND THE
PROMISE OF THE TEN
COMMANDMENTS
TODAY

Adam Hamilton

CONVERGENT
NEW YORK

Published in the United States by Convergent Books,
an imprint of Random House,
a division of Penguin Random House LLC, New York.

CONVERGENT BOOKS is a registered trademark and its C colophon
is a trademark of Penguin Random House LLC.

Library of Congress Cataloging-in-Publication Data
Names: Hamilton, Adam, author.
Title: Words of life / Adam Hamilton.
Description: First edition. | New York : Convergent, [2020]
Identifiers: LCCN 2020025184 (print) | LCCN 2020025185 (ebook) |
ISBN 9781524760540 (hardcover) | ISBN 9781524760557 (ebook)
Subjects: LCSH: Jesus Christ—Teachings. | Ten commandments—
Criticism, interpretation, etc. | Christian life—Biblical teaching. |
Spiritual life—Christianity.
Classification: LCC BV4655 .H29 2020 (print) | LCC BV4655 (ebook) |
DDC 241.5/2—dc23
LC record available at https://lccn.loc.gov/2020025184
LC ebook record available at https://lccn.loc.gov/2020025185

Printed in the United States of America on acid-free paper

convergentbooks.com

2 4 6 8 9 7 5 3 1

First Edition

Title and part opener pages image by boygovideo/Getty Images

Photo credits: page 30: Hunefer/Public domain;
page 41: Ahmed Emad Hamdy/CC BY-SA

With gratitude to W. J. A. Power and Victor Paul Furnish,
emeritus professors of Old Testament and New Testament,
respectively, at Perkins School of Theology, Southern Methodist
University. Their investment in their students, including me,
shaped an entire generation of pastors and gave them the tools to
read the Bible with understanding and to find in it words of life.

Contents

Introduction

It was 2:00 A.M., pitch-dark with a sky full of stars, as we began our hike up the barren mountain. At 7,700 feet, it was not the highest mountain I'd ever climbed. But climbing it in the dark, with no light except the occasional flashlight from a passing guide, was an interesting challenge.

Hundreds of people make this hike to the summit in the darkness every day. They come from all over the world: Christians, Muslims, Jews, and people of other faiths or no faith. They come to what feels like the end of the earth, or perhaps its beginning. They come to hike three hours up the holiest mountain on earth, walking in the dark so they can watch the sun rise from the place where God met Moses and spoke to him the "ten words," as they were originally known—what we know as the Ten Commandments.

How do we know this was *the* mountain? We don't. Scholars have suggested other locations. But from at least the third century A.D., and perhaps long before, people of faith have come to *this* mountain believing it was the biblical

Mount Sinai, Mount Horeb, or simply "The Mountain of God."

As I ascended the mountain in the darkness, I imagined the eighty-year-old Moses making this journey, not once but at least five times. After God delivered the Israelites from slavery in Egypt, Moses led them to this place, for it was here that he had first heard God calling to him from a burning bush, instructing him to lead his people to freedom. Reluctantly, Moses followed God's command, and God used him to liberate the Israelite slaves in dramatic fashion. Three months later, they made camp at the base of Mount Sinai, and Moses was called to meet the Lord on the mountain.

During one of these encounters, shortly after the Israelites arrived at Sinai, God said to Moses:

> I'm about to come to you in a thick cloud in order that the people will hear me talking with you so that they will always trust you. . . . Go to the people and take today and tomorrow to make them holy. Have them wash their clothes. Be ready for the third day, because on the third day the LORD will come down on Mount Sinai for all the people to see. (Exodus 19:9–11)

The writer of Exodus continues:

> When morning dawned on the third day, there was thunder, lightning, and a thick cloud on the mountain, and a very loud blast of a horn. All the people in the camp shook with fear. . . . The LORD came down on Mount Sinai to the top of the mountain. The LORD called Moses to come up to the top of the mountain, and Moses went up. (Exodus 19:16–20)

After telling Moses that the Israelites shouldn't come near the mountain, God sent Moses down again, this time to fetch his older brother Aaron. Two hours down, three hours back up. Finally, with Moses on the mountaintop, Aaron waiting somewhere nearby, and the children of Israel listening below, Exodus tells us, "God spoke all these words":

I am the LORD your God who brought you out of Egypt, out of the house of slavery.

You must have no other gods before me.

Do not make an idol for yourself—no form whatsoever—of anything in the sky above or on the earth below or in the waters under the earth. Do not bow down to them or worship them, because I, the LORD your God, am a passionate God. I punish children for their parents' sins even to the third and fourth generations of those who hate me. But I am loyal and gracious to the thousandth generation of those who love me and keep my commandments.

Do not use the LORD your God's name as if it were of no significance; the Lord won't forgive anyone who uses his name that way.

Remember the Sabbath day and treat it as holy. Six days you may work and do all your tasks, but the seventh day is a Sabbath to the Lord your God. Do not do any work on it—not you, your sons or daughters, your male or female servants, your animals, or the immigrant who is living with you. Because the LORD made the heavens and the earth, the sea, and everything that is in them in six days, but rested on the seventh day. That is why the Lord blessed the Sabbath day and made it holy.

Honor your father and your mother so that your life will be long on the fertile land that the LORD your God is giving you.

Do not kill.

Do not commit adultery.

Do not steal.

Do not testify falsely against your neighbor.

Do not desire and try to take your neighbor's house. Do not desire and try to take your neighbor's wife, male or female servant, ox, donkey, or anything else that belongs to your neighbor. (Exodus 20:1–17)

Within these twenty-one verses, there are 311 words, at least in the Common English Bible's translation above. There is some debate as to how these words should be divided; in other words, what exactly constitutes the Ten Commandments. Jews number them one way, Catholics and Lutherans another, and most Protestants have yet a third way of counting them. In this book, we'll use the division of the commandments used by the Eastern Orthodox Church and most Protestants, focused primarily on the Exodus version.

Note that Exodus calls them "words"—not "commandments." The account also says that they weren't written on stone tablets at first but instead spoken by God from the mountain to his people in the valley below. Only after they were spoken did God write them on stone tablets for Moses to take to the people.

The first four "words" address how the people of Israel, and later all who looked to the commandments for truth, were to live in right relationship with God; how they were to honor, and to avoid dishonoring, God. The remaining six "words" speak to how human beings are to live in right relationship with their parents, with their families, and with their neighbors.

Exodus 32 tells us that the ten words were inscribed onto two stone tablets. It is customary to imagine that the first four commandments, related to honoring God, were on the first tablet. The next six, involving how we relate to our neighbor, were on the second.

Regardless of how one numbers them or which account you are reading from—Exodus or Deuteronomy—my intent in this book is to show that the Ten Commandments are so much more than a relic from history or an ancient set of dos and don'ts. When you look at each of the "words," the principles that lay behind them, and the way Jesus spoke to them and lived them, you'll find that they are far more relevant to your life than you imagined. Far from being burdens meant to rob us of our joy, they are words of life: guideposts and guardrails aimed at helping us experience the goodness and beauty that God intended.

Onerous Rules or Guideposts for a Joy-Filled Life?

Richard Dawkins, perhaps the world's best-known atheist, addressed the Ten Commandments in an opinion piece for *The Guardian:* "Do you advocate the Ten Commandments as a guide to the good life? Then I can only presume that you don't know the Ten Commandments."[1] They were made for a different time and place, he argued. A time when people followed tribal gods, and when those who broke the Sabbath were punished by being stoned to death.

Dawkins has often, and sometimes rightly, criticized elements of the biblical stories and commands, something I've done as well in my book *Making Sense of the Bible.*[2] But in the process of rightly critiquing elements of the biblical narrative, he throws the proverbial baby out with the bathwater. I will hope to make the case in this book that, despite the passages that I would join Dawkins in critiquing, the Ten Commandments, rightly understood, do in fact offer us a guide to the good life.

Sadly, most of the public conversation about the Ten Commandments in recent years has centered on court battles concerning their display in schools, courtrooms, or other government buildings. Often these battles are fought between secularists, who see the posting of the commandments as an endorsement of religion, and certain groups of Christians who believe their removal is another attack on their faith.

The Ten Commandments deserve a place in displays of historic and influential legal codes, like the bas-reliefs at the U.S. Supreme Court, where they are displayed alongside other legal codes from history. But when the Ten Commandments are depicted on their own in government buildings, it is appropriate to ask the purpose of the display. The first four commandments endorse a very particular religion or religions (Judaism and Christianity and, some would argue, Islam, whose Koran mentions the Ten Commandments in passing). They forbid the worship of other gods, misusing the name of Israel's God, and working on the day set apart for rest. It is easy to see why many nonbelievers have taken issue with displays of the Ten Commandments, believing that they endorse a particular religion that millions of people may or may not share.

While some Christians have fought to have the Ten Commandments displayed in such places, many churches seldom teach the Ten Commandments anymore. There was a time when nearly every child who grew up in a Christian home memorized the Ten Commandments. Children were taught the commandments both at home and in church. For generations, they were recited, usually liturgically, in the services of Anglicans and early Methodists. Yet today you would be hard-pressed to find a Christian or a Jew, aside from rabbis and pastors, who can recite all ten commands—much less place them in the proper order.

It is not the public display of the Ten Commandments that seems important to God. They were, after all, originally placed inside the Ark of the Covenant, not on public display. No, what I believe God longs for is that these commandments be inscribed on our *hearts,* understood with our minds, and lived in our daily lives. This is what God said through Jeremiah the prophet: "The time is coming, declares the LORD, when . . . I will put my Instructions within them and engrave them on their hearts" (Jeremiah 31:31,33b).

In the Second Temple period of Judaism (from 516 B.C. to

A.D. 70), it is believed that the Ten Commandments were recited daily in the temple. Every Jewish child would have memorized these commands. In the Gospels, we see that Jesus referred to and practiced the Ten Commandments throughout his ministry. The early church was familiar with the commands, and the apostle Paul referred to most of them throughout his epistles. Across history, the leaders of the church found in these commands the foundations of Christian ethics. They saw that every "thou shalt not" pointed to a life-giving "thou shalt," given by a God who loved them and cared for their well-being. Something important is lost when we forget, or never learn, these essential words God gave us for navigating life.

In this book, we will look at each of the commandments, the history behind them, the way Jesus spoke to them and lived them, and ultimately, how they speak to our lives today. As you read, I'd encourage you to memorize each of the Ten Commandments. You might find it helpful to write them down on a piece of paper or print them from your computer (we're using the Common English Bible throughout this book, unless otherwise noted), tape the list to your bathroom mirror, and say them aloud after you brush your teeth each morning and night. More than memorizing the commandments, however, I'd like you to pray them and seek to live them. In this way, I believe you will find that God's words in these passages serve as an anchor amid the waves of life and our ever-shifting moral seas.

Around 6:00 A.M., as we reached that summit in the desert, the sun finally pushed above the clouds on the eastern horizon, rising above the distant peaks and lighting up the mountains all around us. It was majestic. I sat down beside the small chapel of the Holy Trinity, built from the ruins of a much earlier church, and I prayed once more:

> Lord, help me not only to know your commandments but to live them. Help me to have no other gods before you; help me, that I might not worship anything but you. Help me to hallow your name and not profane it. May I be still, listen, and rest with you on the Sabbath. Make me a blessing to my parents. Help me not to hate or hurt others. Help me to be faithful to my wife in my thoughts, words, and deeds. Help me not to take what isn't mine or to speak falsely of others, and teach me to be content with what I have. In other words, O Lord, help me to love you with all my heart, soul, mind, and strength, and to love my neighbor as I love myself. As you inscribed the commands on stone tablets, I pray that you might inscribe your commands on my heart.

After hours of climbing up the mountain—more than twenty thousand steps, according to my watch—it was time to descend back to the valley where the Israelites were said to have waited for Moses. With my knees and ankles weak, my muscles exhausted, the danger of falling was greater going down than going up. As I descended, I imagined eighty-year-old Moses, carefully clutching the tablets containing those words of life.

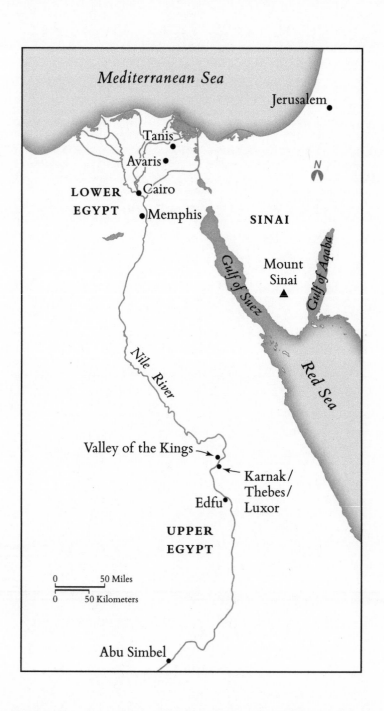

The Call to Love God

Moses then turned around and came down the mountain. He carried the two covenant tablets in his hands. The tablets were written on both sides, front and back. The tablets were God's own work. What was written there was God's own writing inscribed on the tablets.

—Exodus 32:15–16

I

At the Center of It All

Then God spoke all these words:

I am the LORD your God who brought you out of Egypt, out of the house of slavery. You must have no other gods before me.

—Exodus 20:1–3

When I told my wife that I felt compelled to write a book on the Ten Commandments, she gave me a quizzical look and said, "Really, why?"

I was puzzled by the question, so she continued. "I know the Ten Commandments are important. I believe them and try to live them. But I wonder how relevant they are to most people. Most of us don't plan to murder or steal. And who is tempted to worship other gods these days?"

Now it was my turn to raise an eyebrow.

"Okay," she said, "I know—we all struggle with our own false gods. But you know what I mean."

Her response was understandable. At first glance, the

commandments do seem written for a different age ("Thou shalt have no other gods before me. Do not make for yourselves idols") or so basic that we hardly need reminding ("Thou shalt not murder"). But if you dig in a little, understand their historical context, and listen to how Jesus and the apostles interpreted them, you'll find these ancient words speak in profound ways to our lives today. Jesus, in particular, looked behind the rules to the condition of the heart each commandment sought to address. Murder wasn't just the act of killing, he taught. It was resentment and bitterness and hate and the words that spring from them. It wasn't just the act of adultery but desire and the myriad ways sexuality can be misused. We're no longer tempted to worship the gods of the Egyptians and Canaanites, but we still struggle with misplaced devotion and making our pride or career or wealth the god we worship and serve.

But Jesus did more than look at the deeper issues. He had a way of turning the commandments on their head. As I noted in the introduction, for each thou-shalt-not there is an implied and important life-giving thou-shalt. In other words, rightly understood, the commandments don't merely tell us what not to do. They point us, positively, toward how we're meant to live our lives—toward God's will for us in the midst of our deepest struggles. Nowhere is this truer than with the first command, *I am the LORD your God.*

Essential Religion and Ethics for a New Nation

Before we explore the first and most important of the commandments, I'd like to remind you of the context of the Ten Commandments in the biblical story.

It was a famine that led Israel and his children and grandchildren to travel to Egypt in search of food. Beginning around 1800 B.C., they and tens of thousands of other Semitic people migrated to Egypt's lush Nile delta, a region of some five million acres of fertile land. These populations eventually formed a nation within a nation, of which Israel's descendants were one small part.

Later, another wave of immigrants entered the area, a people the Egyptians called the Hyksos (the word meant, in essence, "foreign rulers," though it was used at times with the sense of "shepherd kings"). Also of Semitic origin, they went on to wrest control of the Nile delta, and then much of the rest of Egypt, from Egypt's ruling dynasty. These foreign invaders ruled over much of Egypt until about 1550 B.C., when they were expelled by several succeeding pharaohs marching with their armies from Thebes. Many of the foreigners who remained in Egypt, including the Israelites, were made slaves of the Egyptians.[1]

The Israelites spent generations enslaved and oppressed in Egypt. Among other things, their labor was used to form the mud and straw bricks that went into the massive building projects of the New Kingdom pharaohs. The Israelites did not build the pyramids—these predate the Israelites by many hundreds of years. But from approximately 1550 B.C. to perhaps as late as 1279 B.C., the Israelites were forced to make tens of millions of bricks, which were used to build Egypt's temples, cities, and walls. You'll find them at most ancient archaeological sites from the period, including the magnificent Luxor Temple.

Exodus records that even under oppression, the Israelite population multiplied. It got to the point where the Egyptian pharaoh feared that these foreigners, like the Hyksos before them, might one day pose a threat. So he escalated their oppression. Slaves were made to work harder, keeping the Israelite people under the foot of the powerful Egyptians. Boys born to Israelite women were ordered to be drowned. All of which leads to the story of Moses, found in the opening chapters of the book of Exodus.

When Moses is born, his mother, Jochebed, devises a plan to save him from Pharaoh's decree. It appears she knows of one of Pharaoh's daughters and believes her to be compassionate. Jochebed carefully prepares a basket that can float, then lays her son inside, and places it along the banks of the Nile at the very spot where Pharaoh's daughter comes to bathe. When Pharaoh's daughter finds the baby floating toward her, she takes the child home and adopts him as her own. Raised in Pharaoh's household, Moses would have been educated like a prince, learning Egyptian religion, law, and philosophy.

At the age of forty, Moses goes to observe the Israelite slaves, apparently aware that he was born an Israelite. When he sees their mistreatment at the hands of a particular slave driver, his anger wells up, and he ends up killing the taskmaster. When the act is discovered, Moses is forced to flee to the Sinai. He spends forty years there, no longer a prince in Egypt but now a humble shepherd in the vast desert.

Then, at the age of eighty, Moses hears God speak to him from a bush that's on fire. God says to him, "The Israelites' cries of injustice have reached me. I've seen just how much the Egyptians have oppressed them. So get going. I'm sending you to Pharaoh to bring my people, the Israelites, out of Egypt" (Exodus 3:9–10). With no small amount of resistance, and after exhausting all excuses, Moses does as God commanded. A series of plagues descends upon the Egyptians, and Moses leads the children of Israel to their freedom. He brings them to Mount Sinai, where he first met God in the burning bush, to seek God's direction. Here God will speak to the Israelites from the top of the mountain, giving them the Ten Commandments.

Thousands of people—or millions, if the Exodus text is taken literally—are camped at the base of Mount Sinai when God begins to speak. They have left behind a familiar life with familiar gods. Although they were slaves in Egypt, they at least had food. Now they've risked everything to follow an octogenarian into the barren wilderness, to a place where he claims to have met the God of their ancestors, Abraham, Isaac, and Jacob. Until this day, however, none of them have heard the voice of this God Moses claims to have met.

Standing halfway up the mountain and looking down, it is not hard to imagine their tents and campfires and the hordes of people frozen in terror as they see the smoke and fire bellow on the mountain. Now the God who has delivered them from slavery and who, through Moses, promised them a land flowing with milk and honey, begins to speak:

I am the LORD your God who brought you out of Egypt, out of the house of slavery. You must have no other gods before me (Exodus 20:2).

The Israelites would have known the names of hundreds, perhaps thousands of Egyptian gods. But few of them would have remembered the name of the God of their ancestors

Abraham, Isaac, and Jacob, who lived hundreds of years before them. Moses has told the people of this God whom he met in the burning bush. But now God speaks, introducing himself. "I am the LORD," the text reads in most modern translations, though this is not exactly what the original would have said. The word "LORD," in all capital letters, is used as a stand-in for the Hebrew word "YHWH"—a word most believe is pronounced "Yahweh," though some pronounce it "Jehovah."

While there are many names by which God is called in the Hebrew Bible, this is the most sacred, personal, and at first glance perplexing.[2] We first see it in Exodus 3, when Moses meets God at the burning bush. When God calls Moses to go to liberate the Israelite slaves, Moses asks a pointed question:

> "If I now come to the Israelites and say to them, 'The God of your ancestors has sent me to you,' they are going to ask me, 'What's this God's name?' What am I supposed to say to them?"
>
> God said to Moses, "I Am Who I Am. So say to the Israelites, 'I Am has sent me to you.'" God continued, "Say to the Israelites, 'The LORD, [Yahweh] the God of your ancestors, Abraham's God, Isaac's God, and Jacob's God, has sent me to you.' This is my name forever; this is how all generations will remember me." (Exodus 3:13–15)

In Hebrew, "I Am Who I Am" and "Yahweh" are slightly different forms of the same word: the verb "to be." The name is so important it is found more than 6,400 times in the Old Testament.[3] It is so sacred Jews today will no longer pronounce it. (Hence the replacement word "LORD," which appears in place of "YHWH" throughout the Hebrew Bible.)

For reasons I'll share in chapter 3, I take the name to mean "I am the Source and Sustainer of all that is" or "I am existence itself" or "Everything that exists exists because of me."

Hear again God's introduction to the Israelites: "I am the Source and Sustainer of *everything*. And I am your God. It was I who brought you out of Egypt. It was I who delivered you from your oppression under the Egyptians. I am the one who set you free."

Embedded in God's name is the sweeping claim of scripture: Yahweh is the creator of all things. In the beginning, it was he who spoke the worlds into existence and brought forth life on our planet. He formed human beings, writing the genetic code that makes us who we are. Look at the sunshine, the blue sky, the trees, and the animals. These were all his idea. Think of yourself: your capacity to reason and think; your ability to love and to be loved; the expansion of your lungs as you breathe and the air that fills them. All of these things are gifts from God.

That's what God was revealing to the Israelites when he told them his name. But there was something more he said to them: "I am *your* God."

I Am *Your* God, You Are *My* People

Anyone who commits to study and memorize the Ten Commandments is immediately confronted with a question: What constitutes the first commandment? Jews order the commandments one way. Catholics and Lutherans another. And Eastern Orthodox Christians and most Protestants yet a third way.

For Jews, the first commandment is "I am the LORD

your God who brought you out of Egypt, out of the house of slavery." Christians typically see this not as the lone first commandment but as the prologue or introduction to all the other commandments. For Eastern Orthodox Christians, as well as most Protestants, the first commandment is what God says next: "You must have no other gods before me."

Roman Catholics and Lutherans go further. They consider the first commandment to be "You must have no other gods before me. Do not make an idol for yourself—no form whatsoever—of anything in the sky above or on the earth below or in the waters under the earth. Do not bow down to them or worship them."

Since I am a pastor in the Methodist (Wesleyan/Anglican) tradition, in this book we'll follow the ordering used in my tradition and that of most Protestants and Orthodox Christians. But when it comes to the substance of the text, I think the Jewish people are right in naming the prologue as the first commandment—"I am the LORD your God who brought you out of Egypt, out of the house of slavery." This statement is the premise of all the others. Yahweh is the Source and Sustainer of all that exists, *and* Yahweh has chosen this ragtag band of former slaves to be his people. Interesting to me, the word "your" used in this verse is singular. God is not just the God of the Israelites, but the God of *each of* the Israelites.

This would have been a complete reversal in how they related to the gods of the Egyptians. The Israelites may have believed in those gods, prayed to them, and made sacrifices to them. But at the end of the day, these were *Egyptian* gods. In their providence and will, these gods had made the Israelites the slaves of the Egyptians. The message was clear. To the Egyptian gods, Israelites were second-class, lesser children.

But here was One who claimed to be the source of everything, saying that he *wanted* Israel and was calling these people his own. In claiming to be their God, he was offering his covenant protection and care to them. These were not empty words, for Yahweh had brought them "out of Egypt, out of the house of slavery." Of all the people on earth God might have chosen as his covenant people, he chose a people who were slaves, poor and powerless. God chose the Israelites not because of anything that they had done to merit his kindness but because of the promise he had made to Abraham generations earlier. He chose them because of his covenant love and his compassion and mercy.

This theme winds throughout scripture. God often chooses the powerless, the poor, and the pitiable. God does this because his nature is defined by compassion, mercy, justice, and love.

We see it in God's choice of the elderly Abraham and Sarah, who were too old to have children, to become the parents of a nation. Later, God would bless Ruth, the poor Moabite widow, allowing her to become the great-grandmother of King David. Speaking of David, he was the least impressive of Jesse's eight sons, yet God chose him to become Israel's greatest king. The theme is repeated again and again in scripture, reaching its climax in the New Testament when Jesus, whom Christians believe was God incarnate, spent most of his ministry associating with the uncouth, uneducated, unremarkable. He ate with sinners and tax collectors. He ministered to the physically ill, the mentally broken, and the nobodies. Ultimately, he gave his life on their behalf.

The word Christians most associate with this quality of God's character, this choosing of the unlikely and unworthy, is "grace"—the undeserved love and favor of God extended to us not because of our actions or anything we've done to merit it but solely because God is merciful and kind. Saint Paul famously said of God's saving work in our lives:

> You are saved by God's grace because of your faith. This salvation is God's gift. It's not something you possessed. It's not something you did that you can be proud of. Instead, we are God's accomplishment. (Ephesians 2:8–10a)

Hundreds of times I've had conversations with people who felt they were worthless, insignificant, and unloved, teaching them this truth about God. God knows everything about you. God knows every embarrassing, shameful, or unholy thing you've ever done. God knows the things about you that you beat yourself up for: Are you overweight? Unattractive, at least in your eyes? Do you think you are too stupid or broken or unaccomplished or sinful to be loved and valued? God knows all of this, and God still chooses you, sees you as beautiful and gifted, and *loves* you. God sees not only what you've done and who you've been but what you can do and who you could be.

I recently spoke with a woman who had been picked on, ridiculed, even sexually abused as a teenager. Her whole life has been spent feeling unworthy of anyone's love. As we sat in my office, we reflected on this story of how, throughout the Bible, God decides to honor those whom others have rejected, those who believe they are worthless. He has the power to deliver us from our own land of Egypt—the land where we've grown up being told that we were worthy only of making mud bricks, stepchildren of the gods. As tears streamed down the woman's face, she began to understand for the first time that she was beautiful in God's eyes. She wept as she allowed herself to believe that she was loved, deeply, by God.

This, I think, is what the Israelites understood when they heard these opening words of the Ten Commandments.

What Is a God?

But I also think they were meant to understand that Yahweh was saying, "I am your *God*." Which leads to a question that will be important as we consider the first commandment: What is a God?

On the one hand, ancient Egyptians believed that their gods were benevolent forces who created and sustained the world as they knew it. These forces responded to, looked after, and were somehow involved in the affairs of people. As the Israelites were learning, and as Jews and Christians believe today, all of these forces resided in one God who was the Source and Sustainer of everything that exists. This God is just, compassionate, merciful, loving, righteous, holy, strong and mighty, and much more. God sees humans as his children, his workmanship, the sheep of his pasture, his beloved.

In the Hebrew Bible, there are so many powerful images and metaphors describing God, including a sense of God as protector and provider. Psalm 46:1 comes to mind: "God is our refuge and strength, a help always near in times of great trouble." As the Israelites listened to Yahweh speak, claiming that he was their God, I imagine the sense of peace and gratitude and hope that must have come over them.

As the coronavirus pandemic swept over the world, we all watched as businesses closed, churches stopped holding worship services in person, schools closed for the rest of the school year, and billions of lives came to a standstill as people were ordered to "stay in place." Amid all of this, millions of workers were laid off. LaVon and I told both of our daughters, "Listen, you are our daughters. You are going to be okay. If you need help in any way, we are here for you."

We knew our oldest would continue to be paid and work from home. But our youngest, Rebecca, had just opened a small plant shop and worked on the side at a restaurant and bar. Both would be closed indefinitely, and she would have no income. "I know this is scary," I told her, "but you have nothing to worry about, because we are here. We're family. Whatever you need, we've got you covered." The feeling of belonging, of being loved, of being protected and safe that I was trying to convey to our daughter is similar to what I believe Yahweh was saying to the Israelites.

Whatever challenges you may be facing today, I wonder if you can hear God speaking these words to you: "I am your *God*. I am your companion, your shepherd, your deliverer, your safety, your security, your refuge, and your strength."

No Other Gods

After conveying to the Israelites his name, promising that he will be their God, and reminding them of the deliverance he has already wrought on their behalf, God outlines the terms of his covenant relationship with them. As many have noted, these are not suggestions but religious and ethical requirements governing the covenant relationship between God and his people.

This first commandment calls Yahweh's people to an exclusive relationship with him. *You must have no other gods before me.* Interestingly, God does not say there are no other gods. Only that *you* must have no other gods before or besides me. The Israelites had known and followed a host of other gods. Learning that there was only one God would come later. But here they needed to know only that God had redeemed Israel (a word used to describe purchasing the freedom of another). They no longer belonged to Egypt or Egypt's gods.

Throughout scripture, the biblical authors use human relationships and emotions to describe God. They compare the love God feels for his people to the relationship between a parent and his children, a lover and his beloved, or a husband and his wife. God is said to be a "jealous God" who is offended if Israel gives her love or devotion to another god. This kind of language seems beneath God to some. But it is helpful to remember that the biblical authors, and God, are using language meant to communicate divine truths in words that mortals can comprehend. Take the language of jealousy, of fidelity and infidelity, for example. As a pastor, I've observed on many occasions the pain and heartbreak infidelity causes in marriages. I've also seen the pain of parents who were rejected by their children. These are powerful analogies for teaching both the relationship God seeks from his people in the first commandment and the idea that infidelity to God might actually grieve God.

It's not hard to understand why God would demand an exclusive relationship with his people. When I married LaVon, our pastor asked us if we would be faithful to each other alone "as long as you both shall live." We've spent thirty-eight years fulfilling the covenant we made at our wedding ceremony. In the New Testament, Saint Paul uses the imagery of marriage to describe the relationship Christ has with the church. In the same way, this commandment tells us that God offered fidelity to the Israelites and longed for it from them.

Before considering further this command to exclusivity, it might be helpful to explore the religious context out of which the Israelites had come and the other gods, or suitors, who were vying for their hearts. To that end, I'd like to describe what you would see if you were visiting the great archaeological site of Luxor today.

The Gods of Egypt

Luxor is located 320 miles south of Cairo as the crow flies. Like most major cities in Egypt, it is located on the banks of the Nile. For the first four decades of his life, Moses likely spent most of his time in Luxor, though at the time it would have been known as Waset, the "City of the Scepter." During most of the New Kingdom period—the time when Moses lived—Luxor served as the capital of Egypt. As he grew up, Moses would have worshipped in the Karnak temple complex and accompanied funeral processions to the Valley of the Kings. If a later date for Moses is presumed,[4] he would have walked the halls of the Luxor Temple and Hatshepsut's mortuary temple.

If you visit these archaeological masterpieces today, you'll see that the walls and columns are covered with images of Egypt's most important deities. Often they are accompanied by scenes of the pharaohs bringing offerings to, or being blessed by, the gods. In those days, Pharaoh was considered an intermediary between the gods and mortals, whose offerings and prayers secured the blessings of these same gods. A semidivine being, he ruled over his people on behalf of the gods. If his heart was found righteous at his death, he would enter everlasting life and become a god himself.

The Egyptians believed their deities controlled the natural

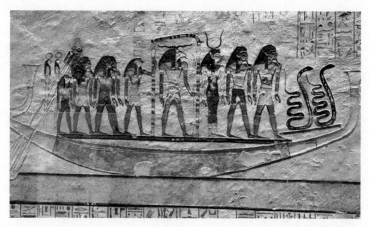

Egypt's god Khnum, center with ram's head, the god who makes humans out of clay, is joined by Hathor, Horus, and others on a funerary barge carrying Pharaoh on his journey into the afterlife. Photo taken by the author in the *Valley of the Kings*

world. They brought the rains, which in turn brought the life-giving floodwaters of the Nile. They opened a woman's womb and ensured the fertility of one's herds and the quality of one's crops. They brought order to the universe and rhythm to daily life. Most were portrayed with the body of a human and, often, the head of an animal that conveyed some part of the deity's character or activity.

Walking through the pharaohs' tombs in the Valley of the Kings or the columned halls of the Luxor or Karnak temples, you'll see bas-reliefs, paintings, and statues of Egypt's chief deities. You'll meet Horus, the falcon, god of the sky. You'll see Hathor, often portrayed as a cow, who was the gentle goddess blessing humanity with love, sexuality, joy, and dancing. You'll meet Hapi, who brought the annual flooding of the Nile River—a blessing to Egypt's agriculture as it covered the earth with its vivifying silt. There is Osiris, god of the underworld, the just judge of the dead. And Isis, Osiris's wife and sister, who gave protection and wisdom to kings and commoners alike.

Many of the tombs depict a scene you may be familiar with: the "weighing of the heart" from the Egyptian Book of the Dead. The scene describes the way Egyptians conceived of the final judgment at death. If one was judged righteous or just, a beautiful afterlife awaited. If not, destruction. In these images, Anubis, the jackal-headed god, weighs the heart of the deceased pharaoh against a feather. Maat sits atop the scale. She is the goddess of truth and justice, and she provides the feather. Thoth, Maat's husband, the god of wisdom and writing, stands ready to record the results. And Ammit is crouched nearby. With the hindquarters of a hippo, the body of a lion, and the head of a crocodile, she stands ready to devour Pharaoh's heart if it is found to be heavier than Maat's feather, ending his quest for everlasting life.

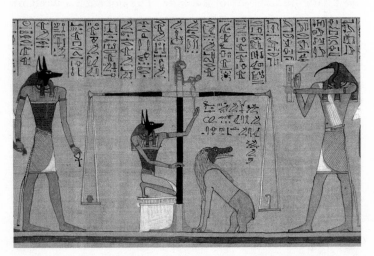

The "weighing of the heart" in the Egyptian Book of the Dead.

The ruler of all of these gods and goddesses in the time of Moses was the mighty Amun-Ra (also spelled Amun-Re).[5] In the New Kingdom period, Amun-Ra was the hidden god, associated with the sun and its life-giving power. Originally worshipped as two separate gods, Amun and Ra, these two deities had been merged into one by the time of Moses. Amun-Ra was the uncreated creator, both powerful and merciful. The Egyptians associated him with fertility and hence often portrayed him with an erection, signifying his role in providing progeny—crops, flocks, and children.

A hymn written to Amun-Ra during the New Kingdom gives a sense of how the Egyptians conceived of him. In it, he is addressed as "Prince of heaven, heir of earth . . . Lord of truth, father of the gods, Maker of men, creator of animals, Lord of the things which are, maker of fruit-trees, Lord of all things that exist!"[6] In a sense, Amun-Ra was to the Egyptians what Zeus was to the Greeks.

Hymns like this give us a sense of the religious devotion the Egyptians had to their deities. It also underscores how Yahweh's call for the Israelites' undivided loyalty might have challenged their deeply held devotion to deities like Amun-Ra. Yahweh's name, I Am Who I Am (I Am the Source and Sustainer), made clear that he, not Amun-Ra, was the Lord of all things that exist.

In that moment beneath Mount Sinai, when the Israelites heard God's voice and saw God's power, they were not at all thinking about going back to Amun-Ra. But later, when life grew difficult in the wilderness, when they had forgotten the oppression they'd known in Egypt—or generations later, when life was good and they no longer needed God—they would return to their old habits, the gods they had known in

Egypt, or the gods who were worshipped by the nations surrounding them in the land of promise.

Throughout much of the Hebrew Bible, we find the Israelites returning to their worship of the old gods or gravitating toward the gods of their neighbors. The grass is always greener, even when it comes to faith. In the Promised Land, the old gods had new names—Baal, Astarte, Molech, Asherah, and Dagon among them. And the lure of these deities was strong. For hundreds of years after Sinai, the Israelites would succumb to worshipping these Canaanite deities, erecting altars and poles on the mountaintops dedicated to them.

The prophets regularly paint a picture of how painful this was to God. God is brokenhearted at Israel's infidelity. But I wonder if God's deeper concern was that he knew the worship of these false gods would ultimately bring his people pain. They were powerless, empty, vapid deities whose paths led away from the Source and Sustainer. Often they led people to act in ways that were abhorrent to God. The apex of such abhorrent behavior was seen on multiple occasions when Israelites, lured by the Canaanite gods, actually sacrificed their own children—burning them alive—in an attempt to secure the god Molech's help.[7] We'll explore these ancient practices further in the next chapter, as we consider the prohibition against making and worshipping idols.

False Gods We Wrestle with Today

At first glance, all this talk of the ancient gods and people offering their children as sacrifices might seem to substantiate my wife's argument that the commandments are far removed from our daily lives. Most of us are not tempted to worship Amun-Ra, nor offer our children as sacrifices.

But there is another sense in which the word "god" might be used. It can also mean that which takes the place of God in our lives. The thing that shapes our identity, values, and actions or serves as our source of security and hope. By this definition, we all have our gods, even atheists and agnostics. And by this definition, we all struggle with the first commandment. We are prone to placing the Source and Sustainer of our lives as a distant second to these other gods.

I know people who believe in God but for whom physical fitness has become their true center. Workouts and nutrition plans are what they eat, sleep, drink, and breathe. They devote more money to fitness than to God and spend more time reading about fitness than reading the scriptures. Their devotion to being healthy is admirable, but it can easily become a god that takes the place of God in a person's life.

Most of these false gods are good and important things that we've given our ultimate devotion to. We've put too much trust in them, expecting them to do what they cannot do. We've placed them on the altar of our hearts, where they were never intended to be.

The first commandment doesn't forbid passions, hobbies, and interests. It forbids putting them above God, worshipping them and serving them in place of him.

In Philippians 3:19 (New Revised Standard Version) Paul wrote of people whose "end is destruction; their god is the belly; and their glory is in their shame; their minds are set on earthly things." What an interesting thought, that for some, their god could be the act of eating. Food is a gift from God, and eating too. A lot of Jesus's best ministry happened over meals, and heaven is described in scripture as a banquet. But

I wonder: When do we cross the line from enjoying food to our belly being our god?

Most people don't notice when they've made something a false god. I think of people who spend hours a day on social media. That may be okay, a way of connecting with loved ones who don't live nearby or of following the news. But at some point, it is possible to become obsessed to such a degree that we have given our hearts to keeping up with social media.

I once knew a man whose love of his job—the corner office, the accolades, and the money—fueled his ego to the point where it edged God out of his life. In the process, it edged out his family too. Caring for his wife and children didn't boost his ego or make him feel excited and energized like his job did. He found it easier and easier to work the long hours, take the business trips, and skip vacations.

One day, after years of living this way, he came home to find a letter from his wife on the kitchen table. She'd taken the kids and wanted a divorce. I'm not sure the man understood what he'd lost until several years later, when the company decided it no longer needed his services, and he was left alone in his mini mansion in suburbia.

As I reflected on this man's life, and those children whose father was absent for much of their formative years, I thought about the god Molech, to whom the Israelites sacrificed their children. There are times when our children, grandchildren, spouses, or parents pay the price for our pursuit of our false gods. The man's story reminded me of the words of Jesus in Matthew 16:26: "Why would people gain the whole world but lose their lives? What will people give in exchange for their lives?"

The Egyptians were said to worship as many as two thousand deities. I suspect we have even more. There are so many false gods to which we might be tempted to give our highest allegiance, our deepest trust. Relationships, clothing, jewelry, success, popularity, health, body size and proportions, image, hobbies, social media, travel, careers, homes, cars, retirement accounts—all of these can become false gods, holding our highest allegiance and having the greatest influence on our thoughts, ideals, and actions. Even our spouse, children, or grandchildren can take the place of God. Good things become distorted and dangerous when we make them the primary focus of our lives.

So many of Jesus's parables address this same tendency. In the parable of the sower (or the soils), Jesus reminds us that there are some who start off well in the Christian life, but then their faith is choked out like wheat that grows among the thorns. He specifically identifies such people as those who hear and respond to the good news of the Kingdom of God, but "the worries of this life and the false appeal of wealth choke the word, and it bears no fruit" (Matthew 13:22b).

The Bible's opening story tells of Adam and Eve eating the forbidden fruit. Do you remember how the serpent tempted them to eat the fruit? It wasn't really about the fruit itself. The temptation came when the serpent told them that if they ate the fruit, they would be like God. The Bible's first recorded temptation was for humans to make gods of ourselves—pride and narcissism, putting ourselves at the center of the universe. There's an acronym you may have heard for what happens when we put the self on the throne of our lives. I've used the phrase several times earlier: "edging God out." Notice the acronym: EGO. In the end, the god we are most likely to put before God is the self.

When I began my study of the Ten Commandments, I

could think of five or six of the commandments I wrestled with in one way or another, but the first commandment didn't come to mind. The more I reflected on what constitutes a false god, however, the more I realized that this might be the commandment I am most tempted to break.

We could fill a book just with examples of false gods, and we'll consider a few more examples as we turn to the second commandment, prohibiting idolatry, in the next chapter. For now, I'd like to end with a reminder of the positive way in which Jesus expressed the essence of this command.

When Jesus was asked what the most important commandment was, he replied not with a prohibition but with a positive mandate: "You shall love the Lord your God with all your heart, with all your soul, with all your mind and with all your strength" (Mark 12:30, NRSV). This is the key to keeping the first commandment. When we love God with all that is within us, we leave no room for false gods.

Loving God and giving our highest allegiance to him enlarges our hearts. It deepens our capacity to love. It transforms our values. It strengthens our commitment. And, by the Holy Spirit's work in us, it results in what Saint Paul called the fruit of the Spirit being produced in us: love, joy, peace, patience, kindness, goodness, gentleness, and self-control. Qualities like these will help us love our spouses more, for example, than if we placed our spouses above God.

This is true of every part of our lives. As we place our trust in God and seek to love him with all our heart, soul, mind, and strength, we become more likely to love our neighbor, to do what is right and just, and to experience the good and joyful life. This commandment is the key to fulfilling all the rest.

I wonder, if God is not in your life, then *what is at the cen-*

ter of your life? What are the false gods you are tempted by? The otherwise good things to which you are tempted to give your highest allegiance, your deepest trust? The things in which you might be tempted to seek your greatest security, to which you might be tempted to devote your time and talent above all else? What, if not God, is the greatest influence shaping your values, ideals, and behavior?

I recently spoke with the CEO of one of the largest hospitals in Kansas City. I told him I had been reflecting on this commandment and what it says about our deepest commitments, what we trust in, what drives us, and our identity. He said, "In my work, the people who walk through our doors at the hospital are usually sick, except those giving birth. And when they are sick, they begin thinking about what really matters. The sicker they are, the less things they thought were important matter. And for those we cannot heal, for whom death draws near, there is only One who remains, in whom they can find hope. I think that's why he calls us to have no other gods before him."[8]

In the Sermon on the Mount, Jesus said to people whose lives were consumed with worry about things like what they would eat and what they would wear, "Desire first and foremost God's kingdom and God's righteousness, and all these things will be given to you as well" (Matthew 6:33). "Desire first and foremost" is a great way of expressing what this commandment calls us to.

When we desire him, his kingdom, and his will first and foremost—when we love him with all that we are and prioritize our faith in and service to him above all else—our capacity to love others grows, our peace and joy increase, and we find life.

What Jesus Might Say to You

My Father says to you, I am *your* God. I have delivered you in the past and will deliver you in the future. I have loved you as a parent loves a child, as a selfless spouse loves their beloved. I want you to have no other gods before me, because when you make something else your god, you are diminished, not enriched. If you love me with all your heart, soul, mind, and strength—if you seek first my kingdom—you'll find so much more than if you'd made something else your god. I plead with you, have no other gods before me.

II

The Idols We Keep

Do not make an idol for yourself—no form
whatsoever—of anything in the sky above or on
the earth below or in the waters under the earth.
Do not bow down to them or worship them.

—Exodus 20:4–5

By way of reminder, the Jewish tradition, along with
Catholics and Lutherans, considers the commandment
above to be part of the first commandment. Most other
Christians view it as the second. There clearly is a sense in
which this commandment forbids devotion and prayer to
gods other than Yahweh. But those who consider it its own
commandment believe it is not merely prohibiting the worship of images and idols of false gods but also prohibiting the
making, praying to, and worshipping of idols that were intended to represent Yahweh himself.

In the second commandment, God emphasized some-
thing that was, and still is, central to Israel's faith: that Yahweh

is not to be portrayed by means of images or statues, for Israel's God is the creator of all things. He transcends the created world, and nothing made by our hands or his (with two
exceptions, as we will see) could adequately represent him.
Hence Israel's religion, alone among the religions of the ancient Near East, would not make images or idols of her God.[1]
With this in mind, let's explore the second commandment.

The Purpose of Idols—Gods You Can See

The temples of ancient Egypt, after which the Israelites' tabernacle and later Solomon's temple were loosely patterned,
were believed to be the palaces of the gods. Walk through the
large outer courts today, and you eventually will come to the
house of the deity. Keep going through this house, and you
will come to another inner room, representing the deity's
throne room. This is the holy of holies. There, on a stand, or
seated on a throne or bench with other deities,[2] is the god
whose house you've entered.

The magnificent temple of Ramesses II at Abu Simbel is
a perfect example from the time of Moses (if one assumes a
thirteenth-century B.C. date for the Exodus, as most mainline scholars do). In the holy of holies, four larger-than-life
statues—idols of Ptah, Amun, Ramesses II, and Re—sit enthroned, awaiting the offerings and prayers of worshippers.
The presence of the pharaoh among the other three deities is
a reminder that the pharaohs were considered semidivine in
their lifetimes and were deified in their deaths.

Though made of stone or wood, the idols in the throne
rooms of temples were thought, in some mystical sense, to
actually embody the deities. A ceremony called "the opening

The holy of holies inside the Great Temple at Abu Simbel. Pharaoh Ramesses II is the second figure from the right, surrounded by other Egyptian gods to whom sacrifices were brought and prayers offered.

of the mouth" appears to have been the means by which the priests brought the idol to life. This ritual included acts of purification, followed by some form of literal opening of the idol's mouth (a chisel was used to further carve or open the mouths of stone idols), clothing the idol, and feeding it. After the ritual, the idol was no longer merely a piece of wood or stone. It was an extension or embodiment of the deity. At this point, the idol would have been placed on its throne in the holy of holies (though at Abu Simbel the deities were carved into place in stone). Rituals were performed and offerings were made to the idol to procure the blessings of the god.

Idols made the invisible gods visible and the intangible gods tangible. At times, the Egyptians took these gods of stone or wood to visit other gods in their temples. These visits were occasions for great festivals. Small boats were built to transport the gods from one part of the Nile to another. The images carved or painted on the temple and burial chamber walls often depict the gods sailing in such boats.

In addition to the temple deities, small statues representing the gods of Egypt or Canaan were crafted, sold, and kept as representations of the deities in the homes of common people. These "household gods" are mentioned at least ten times throughout the Hebrew Bible, and the practice was common throughout the ancient world.

All of this points to the religious life the Israelites knew in Egypt and the context God spoke within when he gave the second commandment. It is for this reason the story in Exodus 32, the making of the golden calf, is not surprising.

The Golden Calf

After God spoke the Ten Words to Moses and the Israelites, Moses remained on the mountaintop for forty days with God—a period that is paralleled by Jesus's forty days in the wilderness during which he fasted, prayed, and was tempted (the pattern for the forty days Christians fast and pray during Lent).[3] Exodus 32 tells us the Israelites became antsy during their own forty-day wait:

> The people saw that Moses was taking a long time to come down from the mountain. They gathered around Aaron and said to him, "Come on! Make us gods who can lead us. As for this man Moses who brought us up out of the land of Egypt, we don't have a clue what has happened to him." (Exodus 32:1)

When they ask Aaron to make them "gods," the Hebrew word is *elohim,* which, while a plural word for gods, is also used of Israel's God in what is known as the "majestic" or "divine" plural. Perhaps a better translation (and one often found in a footnote on this passage) is "Come on! Make us a *God* who can lead us." They wanted Aaron to make them an idol of Yahweh like the idols that the Egyptians had of their gods.

So what did Aaron do?

> Aaron said to them, "All right, take out the gold rings from the ears of your wives, your sons, and your daughters, and bring them to me." So all the people took out the gold rings from their ears and brought them to Aaron. He collected them and tied them up in a cloth. Then he made a metal image of a bull calf, and the people declared, "These are your gods, Israel, who brought you up out of the land of Egypt!" (Exodus 32:2–4)

Once again, the word translated here as "gods" is *elohim,* the standard word for God throughout the Hebrew Bible. Many scholars believe that the better translation is "This is your God, Israel, who brought you up out of the land of Egypt." Note that Aaron did not make multiple images or idols; there was only one metal calf. (Nehemiah 9:18, in recounting this story, makes it clear that the people made the golden calf to represent their God, not multiple gods.)

After hearing the people proclaim that the golden calf was their God, we read in Exodus 32:5, "When Aaron saw this, he built an altar in front of the calf. Then Aaron announced, 'Tomorrow will be a festival to the LORD!'" (Remember, when you see "LORD" in all capital letters in the Hebrew

Bible, the Hebrew word is "Yahweh.") The altar in front of the calf would be used at a festival for Yahweh, indicating that the golden calf was meant to represent him.

But this act angered God, who sent Moses back down the mountain carrying the two stone tablets on which the Ten Commandments were written. When Moses arrived at the camp, he found the people singing and dancing. In his anger, Moses threw the stone tablets to the ground, breaking them apart, and then he seized the calf and destroyed it in the fire. When he questioned Aaron, his brother, about the making of this calf, Aaron said he was just doing what the people asked for, forging a God that would go before them to the Promised Land. They could trust in Yahweh, Aaron seemed to believe, provided they could see him.

Two things are clear in this episode: First, humans prefer to worship gods they can see—for most of us, *seeing is believing*. And second, God rejected idols or images made to represent him; nothing created either by God or by humans can adequately express the glory of God. For God, *believing is seeing*.

I'm writing this chapter in the midst of a fierce Kansas thunderstorm. It's dark outside and the lightning is glorious and terrifying. The thunder is giving my dog a panic attack. The hailstones make a tympanic wall of sound as they strike the furniture on my back porch. And the wind and downpour of rain round out the symphony. These naturally occurring phenomena have always been considered reflections of the glory of God. The countless stars in a clear night sky too. The beauty of all creation was the handiwork of a God whose glory transcended it all.

In 1954, Graham Sutherland was commissioned to paint a portrait of Winston Churchill. Originally intended to hang

in Parliament, it would be presented to Britain's prime min-
ister for his eightieth birthday as he was nearing the end of his
second term. Sutherland was a gifted artist, and while his
portrait of Churchill was hailed by some, it was considered
"disgusting" by others. When Churchill saw it, he was *deeply*
disappointed. A year after the portrait's presentation, it was
later reported, Lady Churchill cut the painting into pieces
and burned it.

Sutherland was one of Britain's finest artists, but even he
could not convey the person Churchill believed himself to be.
It's a lesson in ego and art, perhaps, but when it comes to
God, what artist and what medium could possibly capture the
glory and majesty of the one who spoke the universe into
existence? This is why God commands the Israelites not to
create idols to represent him.

Be that as it may, the Israelites continued to struggle, as
humans have throughout time, with the tendency to create
and worship physical gods. Isaiah 40, written centuries after
the time of Moses, addresses this phenomenon in one of the
most oft-cited passages in the Bible. Permit me to offer a
slightly lengthier excerpt from this chapter, as it conveys so
powerfully Isaiah's argument against making images or idols
of God:

To whom then will you liken God,
or what likeness compare with him?
An idol?—A workman casts it,
and a goldsmith overlays it with gold,
and casts for it silver chains. . . .
It is [God] who sits above the circle of the earth,
and its inhabitants are like grasshoppers;
who stretches out the heavens like a curtain,

and spreads them like a tent to live in;
who brings princes to naught,
and makes the rulers of the earth as nothing. . . .
To whom then will you compare me,
or who is my equal? says the Holy One.
Lift up your eyes on high and see:
Who created these?
He who brings out [the stars] and numbers them,
calling them all by name . . .
Have you not known? Have you not heard?
The LORD is the everlasting God,
the Creator of the ends of the earth.
He does not faint or grow weary;
his understanding is unsearchable.
He gives power to the faint,
and strengthens the powerless.
Even youths will faint and be weary,
and the young will fall exhausted;
but those who wait for the LORD shall renew their
    strength,
they shall mount up with wings like eagles,
they shall run and not be weary,
they shall walk and not faint. (Isaiah 40:25–26b,28–31,
    NRSV)

While God's glory was not meant to be represented by idols, in his mercy, he did allow for material things to be crafted to represent his presence among his people. The tabernacle and later the temple were examples of this provision, as was the Ark of the Covenant.

The Ark of the Covenant:
An Empty Throne?

During those forty days when Moses was on the mountain-top and the Israelites were fretting down below, Exodus 25 and 26 record that God gave instructions for Moses to make a special box called the Ark of the Covenant. This box was to be made of acacia wood covered in gold and measure about four feet wide, twenty-seven inches deep, and twenty-seven inches tall—about the size of what used to be called "hope chests." On either end were carvings of cherubim, winged creatures. These creatures show up frequently in a variety of places in Egyptian art and sometimes constituted the arms of Pharaoh's throne. The box could be opened, and its purpose was to store the two tablets containing the Ten Commandments. Some have seen the ark as God's footstool, but it seems more likely that it was meant to represent God's symbolic throne.

The top of the ark was called the "mercy seat." But unlike other thrones of gods we know of from the ancient Near East, the throne for Israel's God had no image of God, no idol enthroned upon it. The throne was not vacant. No, the Israelites believed that wherever the ark was, God was present there. But the empty space atop the throne, between the two cherubim, was intended to remind Israel that Yahweh's appearance is inconceivable and his glory incomprehensible. In fact, God told Moses, no one could see the fullness of his glory and survive the experience (Exodus 33:20).

Listen again to the second commandment, *Do not make an idol for yourself—no form whatsoever—of anything in the sky above or on the earth below or in the waters under the earth. Do not bow down to them or worship them.* In its historical and religious context, we see just how revolutionary this commandment was, and what it was seeking to convey about the glory of God.

In a sense the Ark of the Covenant, the tabernacle (the tent of meeting, Israel's portable shrine), and later the temple may have been God's nod to our need for something tangible that might represent, if not God himself, at least his presence in the midst of his people. In a sense, that is what church buildings, Bibles, crosses, candles, and even the bread and the wine of Eucharist are for Christians today. They are not idols meant to be worshipped. They are not meant to be wholly adequate representations of the glory of God. But they can be, like the ark and the tabernacle, powerful reminders that God is with us.

Of all the commandments, we might be tempted to think that this one is the least relevant for us. But let's consider a few of the ways that Christians violate this commandment today.

When Faith Becomes an Idol

In the introduction to this chapter, I mentioned the two senses in which we might read this commandment. The first sense is closely linked to the first commandment and involves worshipping false gods in the form of material objects. The second is making material things representing God and treating them as though they were God.

Regarding the latter, allow me to name some things that are meant to remind us of God, or in some way represent God, but that we can come to put in the place of God. We would never intentionally do this. To even say it sounds absurd. But I've known many people who have done just this.

I've known people who came to worship their church buildings more than the God for whose worship they were built. I recall a community where a quaint Methodist church had stood for over one hundred years. It was old enough that it still had outhouses out back. Then an amazing thing happened—the little community became a suburb of a larger city. Thousands of new people moved into town. New neighborhoods sprang up, and new schools were built.

The bishop of that area suggested that if the church wanted to reach the new residents, it should relocate three miles east and create a space with indoor plumbing and room for children. The congregation said no. The bishop pleaded with them, concerned that there was no church of any denomination in this community, and people needed what the church could offer. He even offered grants to relocate. But the people refused. Why? Because they loved that old building. They had so many wonderful memories inside its walls. And they rather liked the congregation the size it was, with all their closest friends sitting in their favorite pews. Perhaps it's too harsh to say that these people had made an idol of their building and their community, but I think it helps us see a modern idol Christians sometimes worship.

Even the Bible has served as an idol to some Christians I've met. God speaks through scripture, but the Bible is not God. It is intended to be not worshipped but read, studied, interpreted, and lived. The Bible was written by human beings living in particular times and places, reflecting upon their experiences of God and their sense of God's word to them and their communities. Though inspired by the Spirit, the text was also shaped in response to the world in which its human authors lived and in the light of their life experiences. God spoke to, and through, the authors of scripture. Through them, and by the Spirit, he continues to use their words to speak to us today. But too often, Christians come to love their Bible more than the God to whom it bears witness. Other times they ascribe to the Bible attributes that belong to God alone.

Some Christians I know idolize their pastors or youth ministers or choir directors or Sunday-school teachers or favorite Christian writers. Often these persons have played such an important role in our lives; from them we have felt God's love and through them we have heard God speak. If we're not careful, we can come to love God's human instruments more than the God who speaks through them.

I've seen this happen with people who don't read the Bible, only their favorite Christian author. I've also observed it when Christians stay home from church when their beloved preacher has the Sunday off. If that preacher fails or falls short or otherwise disappoints, their faith might be dashed, because their faith was in the preacher, or the youth director, or the Sunday-school teacher, more than in God.

Missions, music, social justice, the fight for inclusion, environmental ministry, teaching children, and a hundred other good things that we might do *for* God can easily take the place *of* God in our lives. In the same way, I've known Christians who made politics and politicians an idol. As we noted in chapter 1, there is no shortage of other idols, inanimate objects—cars, retirement portfolios, material possessions—to which we can give our highest devotion in place of God.

Jesus speaks frequently of one idol in particular: money. "No one can serve two masters. Either you will hate the one and love the other, or you will be loyal to the one and have contempt for the other. You cannot serve God and wealth" (Matthew 6:24). Jesus was speaking to first-century peasants who struggled with making their wealth their god. How much more do we wrestle with this as people living in twenty-first-century America?

That is why God has given us the gift of the second commandment. *Do not make idols for yourselves.*

The Image of the Invisible God

The second commandment prohibits us, as humans, from making idols or forms that represent God, or things that take the place of God. Yet the Bible tells us of two ways in which God has made his image visible.

Consider Colossians 1, verses 15 and 19: "The Son is the image of the invisible God, the one who is first over all creation. . . . [A]ll the fullness of God was pleased to live in him." John's majestic prologue to his Gospel refers to Jesus as "the Word," God's self-disclosure or revelation, and then notes, "And the Word became flesh and lived among us, and we have seen his glory, the glory as of a father's only son, full of grace and truth" (John 1:14). Later in that same Gospel text, Jesus says, "I and the Father are one" (John 10:30) and "If you have really known me, you will also know the Father" (John 14:7). He is the incarnation of God—not an idol made of stone or wood or precious metal but God enfleshed. The glory of God, come to us in person. He is not an idol we have made but a reflection of the image of God that God himself gave to us that we might see, we might know, and we might believe.

The second form in which God has placed his image is

you and me. We read this in the opening words of scripture: "God created humanity in God's own image, in the divine image God created them, male and female God created them" (Genesis 1:27). We were made in God's image. We are meant to reflect God's glory. Our capacity to do that is marred by our propensity to turn away from God's path. But when we walk with Christ, when we seek to do his will, when we love God with our whole heart and we love our neighbor as we love ourselves, we actually reflect the image of God.

Debbie is a member of the church I serve and a cashier at a nearby grocery store. Not long ago, she told me that she'd witnessed a miracle that week. A woman came to her register with a shopping cart full of food, her monthly grocery run. But as Debbie was ringing things up, she noticed the woman began setting items back in her cart to return to the shelves. When Debbie hit "total," the bill came to about $250.

The woman handed Debbie her EBT (Electronic Benefit Transfer) card, provided by the state of Kansas to assist low-income people. The card indicated she had only $188 on her account. She stood in line and began to weep, apologizing and pulling things back to put away. Just then the woman behind her spoke up and said, "Please let me buy your groceries this time." She gave her credit card and bought $250 worth of groceries for the other woman. When Debbie had finished charging the credit card, all three of them were crying.

I don't know if the woman who paid the grocery bill was Christian, Jewish, Muslim, Hindu, Buddhist, or an atheist. What I do know is that in that moment she reflected the image of God. She didn't know the woman she was helping. But she showed compassion for her and did an act of pure grace.

Don't make for yourself an image that you will bow down to. But if you want to see God, look to Jesus, who is the image of the invisible God. And don't forget, you were created in the image of God as well. When you love your neighbor as yourself, others can see God in you.

What Jesus Might Say to You

You were made in the image of the invisible God. And I came to reflect his presence, power, and love to you, that you, in turn, might reflect his image to others. You most clearly reveal his image in you when you demonstrate selfless love. Don't put anything you can see on a pedestal, allowing it to replace the God from whom all blessings flow; not your political leaders, your heroes, your family, or even your preacher. Don't worship the things that you can see and feel and touch. And don't let your career, your dreams, your possessions, or your aspirations replace God on the throne of your life. No one can serve two masters. Instead, worship him alone, and you will have found the life you were created to live.

III

"I Swear to God!"

Do not use the LORD your God's name as if it
were of no significance; the LORD won't forgive
anyone who uses his name that way.

—Exodus 20:7

Has anyone ever tried to steal your identity? It happens to
me on a near weekly basis on Facebook. Some years
ago, I created what Facebook calls an "organizational page"
on which I post short reflections, news, and updates for my
congregation and people who read my books. I also maintain
a private page for my immediate family. Several times a
month, however, someone will create a fake Adam Hamilton
profile on Facebook, copy photos from my personal and organizational pages, and send friend requests to the people
who follow my organizational account.[1]

If someone accepts a friend request from the person claiming to be me, the fake Adam Hamilton will begin sending
them messages asking how "I" might pray for them. Eventu-

ally, the scammer starts asking the person for money for "mission projects" in Africa. Most people figure out the scam, as the fake Adam Hamilton usually writes in stilted English. I report these fraudulent accounts to Facebook as soon as I hear about them, and Facebook removes them within a few days of their creation.

These scammers frustrate me. They seek to defraud people in my name. I've reported them to the authorities, but law enforcement can't do anything until a crime has been committed. Even then, they show little ability to address fake social media accounts. Because of these accounts, I never ask persons to be my friends on Facebook, and I tell my congregation that if they receive a friend request from someone claiming to be me, it is a fraudulent account. The thought of someone being taken advantage of or hurt in my name on social media really angers me.

In the third commandment, God says to the Israelites, "Do not use the LORD your God's name as if it were of no significance; the LORD won't forgive anyone who uses his name that way." In the New Revised Standard Version it reads, "You shall not make wrongful use of the name of the LORD your God, for the LORD will not acquit anyone who misuses his name." The King James Version is what most are familiar with: "Thou shalt not take the name of the LORD thy God in vain; for the LORD will not hold him guiltless that taketh his name in vain."

Each of these translations captures a slightly different interpretation of this important commandment. We often think of this commandment as forbidding "cussing," but as we take a closer look at the historical context, we'll find that the commandment likely addressed using God's name in ways similar to how the scammers on Facebook use mine. As he does with the other commands, we'll see that Jesus calls us not merely to avoid doing what is prohibited by the commandment but to positively "hallow" God's name—not only in our words but also in our actions.

The Power of God's Name

As I noted in chapter 1, I take God's name, "Yahweh," to mean something like "I am BEING itself." Or "Everything that exists derives its existence from me." Or, perhaps best, "I am the Source and Sustainer of *everything*." God's name speaks to God's identity and nature and the relationship of God to everything that exists. His name is a sweeping claim about who God is and how we are meant to relate to him.

Saint Paul seemed to capture this same sense of God's name when he spoke to the philosophers of ancient Athens, saying of God (while quoting a Greek poet), "In him we live and move and have our *being*" (Acts 17:28, NRSV). The twentieth-century existentialist theologian Paul Tillich described God as the "Ground of Being." By this name, God makes clear that *everything* derives its existence from and is sustained by Yahweh.

God's name, "Yahweh" (and its abbreviated form, "Yah"), appears more than six thousand times in the Hebrew Bible, more than all other names for God *combined*. Yet in many English translations, "Yahweh" never once appears in the text except in a footnote or in the translation notes. Sadly, translators have replaced "Yahweh" with "the LORD," which misses the power of the name and its frequent use by the biblical authors.

Consider for a moment all of the familiar passages that contain "the LORD." I'll quote a few, citing them as they are actually written. Psalm 23 (King James Version) begins, "Yahweh is my shepherd, I shall not want." It ends, "And I will dwell in the house of Yahweh forever." The most important creed of Judaism, the Shema Israel in Deuteronomy, says, "Israel, listen! Our God is Yahweh! Only Yahweh! Love Yahweh your God with all your heart, all your being, and all your strength" (Deuteronomy 6:4–5, KJV). Those famous words from Micah 6:8 (NRSV) actually read, "What does Yahweh require of you but to do justice, and to love kindness and to walk humbly with your God?" There are more than six thousand other verses like this.

So why do translators substitute "the LORD" (with "LORD" in all caps) for "Yahweh"? The practice began among the Jewish people in response to the very commandment we're considering. Sometime before or near the time of Jesus, there developed a great concern that a person might inadvertently violate the third commandment by misusing God's name. It was deemed better not to say the name at all. Written Hebrew has no vowels. Scribes use dots or points between the consonants to signify what vowel sound should be made. Long after the time of Moses, when scribes copying the Hebrew Bible came to the divine name, "Yahweh," they would insert the vowel points for the Hebrew word *adonai,* which means "lord" (authority, ruler, owner, master, leader). They did this to remind readers not to speak God's name but to substitute the word *adonai* for "Yahweh." Thus began the practice of substituting the word "LORD" for "Yahweh."

Because the Jewish people stopped speaking the name, no one is quite sure how it should be pronounced. When the vowel pointing for *adonai* is pronounced with the consonants for "YHWH," one comes up with "Jehovah" or "Yehovah." It's unlikely that this is how God's name was actually pronounced, though some argue that it was. Most scholars believe the original pronunciation of the name was "Yaw-way."

Ultimately both Jews and Christians, when translating the Hebrew Bible from Hebrew to English, follow the same principle: Instead of transliterating God's name into English as "Yahweh," they substitute for this name "the LORD." For the rest of this book, when the English translation has substituted "the LORD" for "Yahweh," I will usually offer the word "Yahweh," as the Hebrew actually has it. (For example, *Do not use Yahweh your God's name as if it were of no significance; Yahweh won't forgive anyone who uses his name that way.*)

Why should we care about what seems an esoteric concern about a cryptic Hebrew word for God? Because in this name, God was seeking to help us know that our lives, and all that exists, are utterly and completely dependent upon him; he is Yahweh. And we should care because this is the name God has said his people would know him by.

I would argue that any name we might use for Yahweh should be treated with reverence and respect—be it "the LORD," "God," or, as Christians, "Jesus Christ" or "the Holy Spirit." This commandment reminds us that God takes personally how we use, or misuse, his name. Do you revere God? Then don't use God's name as though it were of no significance.

In the rest of this chapter I'd like to mention several applications of this command to our lives today, then to turn to how Jesus gave us a new way of understanding and living it.

Profanity

My family wasn't active in church when I was little, but somehow they managed to instill the third commandment into my mind in this form: *Thou shalt not take the name of the Lord thy God in vain.* To take God's name in vain, it was implied, meant using profanity, whether that profanity mentioned God or not. I seem to recall my mother threatening to "wash out your mouth with soap" if I used profanity, though thankfully I don't remember her ever carrying through on this threat.

The word "profanity," along with the word "profane," comes from the Latin *pro* (outside) and *fanum* (temple). It meant, literally, taking something holy from within a temple and throwing it out of the temple. In other words, debasing or desecrating something holy; stripping something of its sacred character.

What does it look like to profane and desecrate God's name, "Yahweh" (or any other name representing God)? At the very least, it would mean to use it without reverence, to use it casually, as if it didn't matter. The Hebrew word translated as "in vain" in the King James Version or "of no significance" in the Common English Bible is the word *lassaw*, which means "to consider lightly." While the command specifically speaks of the name "Yahweh," again I would argue that it applies to the other words we use for Yahweh or his Son—words like "God" or "Lord" or "Jesus." Do you ever use any of these words in a way that is irreverent, rendering them of no significance?

On a recent trip to the grocery store, I ran into a five-year-old boy who is a part of the church I serve. His mother was there too. As I was speaking to them, the little boy saw something that caught his attention and exclaimed, "Oh my God!" His mother looked a bit embarrassed that her son had just used the word "God" in this way in front of the pastor, aware that this might be seen as a reflection of how she used the word "God" in her own home. But the five-year-old was in good company. I've known many adults, including a few preachers and even a bishop or two, who used this same figure of speech. Others use Jesus's name as an expletive. "Jesus Christ!" they say in anger or frustration. I've also heard people exclaim, "Jesus H. Christ!" when they stub their toe, hit their finger while hammering a nail, or drive a golf ball into the rough. (What does that *H* stand for, anyway?)

If you use "God," "Jesus," "Lord," or any other word for God in a way that does not reflect reverence for God, I'd encourage you to stop. This commandment, at the very least, makes clear that this is something that displeases God.

But while profanity is the most obvious application of the commandment today, it is actually the least serious of the violations of this command, and it is unlikely that "cussing" is what Moses or God was really thinking about when the commandment was given. I suspect most ancient people would not have considered using the names of their gods in such careless ways. So let's take a deeper look at the ways in which we use God's name.

Promise Keeping and Truth Telling

Many scholars have suggested that the primary intent of this commandment had to do with the practice of swearing oaths in the name of God. It called the ancient Israelites (and us) to keep their promises and tell the truth.

In the ancient world, when people made promises or were seeking to emphasize that they were telling the truth, they would swear by the name of their god. We still do the same thing. In a courtroom, it used to be common for people to "swear to tell the truth, the whole truth, and nothing but the truth, *so help me God*." Even now you'll hear people accompanying statements that might be hard to believe with the exclamation "I swear to God!" The invoking of God's name is a way of offering a guarantee that we are telling the truth.

We also invoke God's name when making important promises. One example from politics is the presidential oath of office. The oath, administered by the chief justice of the Supreme Court, is usually sworn on a Bible as the incoming president recites these words: "I do solemnly swear (or affirm) that I will faithfully execute the office of president of the United States, and will to the best of my ability, preserve, protect, and defend the Constitution of the United States." Most recent presidents have actually placed their hands on *two* Bibles. Over the years, many presidents have added the words "I will, so help me God" to the end of the oath, though it is not technically part of it.

Consider, too, the wedding vows that most people swear. In my tradition, the vows are (I'll use my name and my wife's name) "In the name of God, I, Adam, take you, LaVon, to be my wife. To have and to hold from this day forward. For better, for worse. For richer, for poorer. In sickness and in health. To love and to cherish as long as we both shall live. This is my solemn vow."

When I officiate weddings, I remind the couple that these

promises are not only to each other but also to God. Truth telling and promise keeping are essential to a healthy marriage. And two things that are sure to kill a marriage are infidelity and dishonesty. We need both promise keeping and truth telling to make our most intimate of relationships work.

The Torah itself makes clear this connection between truth telling and promise keeping and the third commandment. We see this in *The Jewish Study Bible*'s translation of the third commandment: "You shall not swear falsely by the name of the Lord your God; for the Lord will not clear one who swears falsely by his name."[2] Leviticus 19:12 echoes the same: "You must not swear falsely by my name, desecrating your God's name in doing so; I am Yahweh." And Numbers 30:2 draws out the point more practically: "When a man makes a solemn promise to Yahweh or swears a solemn pledge of binding obligation for himself, he cannot break his word. He must do everything he said." These texts make clear that misusing Yahweh's name is about not living up to the commitments we've made in our relationships with other people.

I've officiated many funeral services where friends of the deceased say of their loved one, "Their word was their bond." This is usually said of older adults—the phrase doesn't get used as often today—but perhaps we should reintroduce it to upcoming generations. The idea of always keeping our promises regardless of the cost often seems to have been lost. But to be a person of character includes promise keeping and truth telling.

Having considered a couple applications of the third commandment, let's turn now to how Jesus interpreted and applied it. Once again, Jesus's teaching moves from the "thou shalt not" of the commandment to a positive ethic for how we're meant to live our lives, an ethic that is ultimately life-giving.

Jesus, Truth Telling, and Oath Keeping

Thus far, we've learned that this commandment has to do with not using God's name in a way that profanes it, with not representing God in a way that defames his name, and with staying true to the promises we've made. Jesus's teaching is consistent with these same concerns, but in the Sermon on the Mount, he takes up the issue of promise keeping and carries it even further:

> You have heard that it was said to those of ancient times, "You shall not swear falsely, but carry out the vows you have made to Yahweh." But I say to you, Do not swear at all, either by heaven, for it is the throne of God, or by the earth, for it is his footstool, or by Jerusalem, for it is the city of the great King. And do not swear by your head, for you cannot make one hair white or black. Let your word be "Yes, Yes" or "No, No"; anything more than this comes from the evil one. (Matthew 5:33–37, NRSV)

In Jesus's day, people developed carefully crafted oaths sworn by heaven, or by the temple, or the gold in the temple, with the intent of reassuring the other person that they would fulfill the oath (think statements like "I swear on my mother's grave!") or perhaps leaving wiggle room to get out of the promise. But Jesus challenged them, "Enough with the crafty promises! Just be a person of your word." Sometimes keeping your word is costly, but keep it anyway. Concerning this, Psalm 15 notes, "Who can live in your tent, Yahweh? . . . Someone who keeps their promise even when it hurts" (Psalm 15:1 and 4c).

We live in a time when truth seems hard to come by and promises are often not kept. We've seen national leaders of both political parties tell bald-faced lies with no repercussions. We no longer find it surprising when someone goes back on their word after their promise becomes costly. But people of integrity continue to tell the truth. They do the right thing even when it is costly. They do not say one thing and do another.

Years ago, I visited a large church in Houston, seeking to learn from its staff. I spoke with the executive pastor and asked him to tell me about his senior pastor. I'll never forget how he described his senior pastor. He said, "The people who know him the best respect him the most." By this he meant that those who watched his senior pastor's behavior most closely knew that he "practiced what he preached." No doubt you can think of people from your own life who fit that description.

Years ago, I needed to rebuild the deck on my house. A neighbor suggested I call Marty, a master carpenter and craftsman. I did, and I have been using him ever since. Marty is unassuming, kind, smart, honest, and one of the hardest-working guys you'll ever meet. He'll tell you he won't be the fastest guy to do the job—he often works by himself—but no one will do the job better. He never cuts corners. He knows the right way to fix things. He gives me a price up front and never charges me more. The quality of his workmanship is outstanding. From years of working with him, I've come to know that I can trust Marty. And I know when he suggests that something be repaired, it's not because he's trying to make a buck but because he genuinely cares for me and wants what is best for me and my family. His contracts and work are not explicitly done in the name of God, but I believe his faith shapes the man he is, and that, in turn, shapes the way he does his work.

This is the true test of character. Telling the truth and keeping your promises is not hard when it costs you nothing. But real character is seen when telling the truth or keeping our promises comes at a price. Are you willing to tell the truth, and willing to keep your promise, even when it costs you something?

There is one final way I'd like us to think about this commandment and how it applies to us. We learned in the last chapter that while we're not to make images of God to worship, God created humanity in his image, and we are meant to reflect his image to one another. As God's people, we bear the name of God. And we can speak about God not only through our words but through the way we live our lives.

Misrepresenting God

Have you ever noticed on the backs of certain commercial trucks a decal saying, "How's my driving?" followed by a phone number? The decals are there to hold the drivers accountable and to help the company know if it has an unsafe driver behind the wheel of one of its trucks. I once heard the CEO of a company contact one of his employees who was speeding in the company van, weaving in and out of traffic and driving aggressively. He told the driver, "When you are driving the van with our company logo on the side, you are representing us. What you've told everyone you pass, every driver who feels you were unsafe or were rude in how you drive, is that we as an organization are unsafe, aggressive, and rude. You and your driving may be the only thing people know about us, and this kind of driving is not okay."

The Israelites were God's chosen people, called to be a "light for the nations." They were meant to represent and reveal God's character and will. Later Jesus said the same of his disciples, the church. "You are the light of the world," he told them, "a city built on a hill that cannot be hid. . . . Let your light shine before others, so that they may see your good works and glorify your Father who is in heaven" (Matthew 5:14–16, NRSV).

At the church I pastor, the United Methodist Church of the Resurrection, we have a decal people can put on their car bumper or window identifying the car's occupants as members of Resurrection—a circle with a portion of the United Methodist cross and flame within, and our web address: cor .org. This is a wonderful way to share your faith, except when we drive or act while driving in a way that doesn't reflect well upon our faith. The same is true when we wear crosses around our necks or make clear to our coworkers that we are people of faith. As people who identify ourselves with God, our lives speak and we witness to our faith as much by our actions as by our words.

Representing God with Our Words

Pastors and teachers who regularly speak, preach, and teach in the name of God are regularly in danger of violating this commandment. Each week, the preacher stands in the pulpit declaring the "counsel of God" (see Acts 20:27). Yet they (and I include myself here) are mere mortals whose theological reflections are at times faulty. Sure, we have the scripture to guide us. But the scripture must be interpreted and applied, and that is where the challenge comes in. The implications of this are that as we preach, write, or teach, we have ample opportunity to violate the third commandment, misusing God's name or misrepresenting God's heart, character, and will. Are any of us, with our three pounds of gray matter inside our head, really up to comprehending the mind of God? It has been said that if you have fully understood God, your God is way, way too small.

With thousands of preachers, teachers, and theologians writing and speaking on behalf of God, it can sound like the aftermath of the Tower of Babel, with authorities professing very different understandings of who God is, how God works, and what constitutes God's will. I know Christians whose God seems clearly to be a Tea Party Republican, and others whose God is clearly a left-wing Democrat. One hundred miles from where I live, congregants at the infamous Westboro Baptist Church carry their signs to funerals, churches, and public gatherings proclaiming who God hates. More recently, I think of the preachers and rabbis who blamed gay and lesbian people for provoking God to send the novel coronavirus.

I also think of the kind of half-truths well-meaning Christians sometimes say, hoping to be helpful or comforting to those who have experienced tragedy. When someone loses a job, is diagnosed with cancer, or loses a close friend or family member, inevitably a Christian friend will seek to console them with the words "It must have been the will of God." I recall speaking with a parent who told me that she had stopped believing in God after the death of her son, several years earlier. It wasn't his death that had turned her from God. It was the people who told her that her son's death was God's will. She asked, "Why would I ever love and serve a God who killed my five-year-old son?"

One wonders how God must feel hearing this cacophony of voices, some speaking in ways that grossly misrepresent him. This is not new, of course—the false prophets of Israel did the same. But the challenge is that the false prophets never believe they are false prophets. They believe they are rightly interpreting and proclaiming the will of God. Often they can point to chapter and verse in the Bible to support their claims. I find it interesting that even the devil quotes scripture when seeking to tempt Jesus. That alone should leave us a bit cautious about declaring, "Thus sayeth the Lord."

Honoring God by Our Actions

Some years ago, a study was done of young adults who were not actively involved in any form of church. When asked why they were not involved, their top response was the hypocrisy they saw in self-identified Christians. It was Gandhi who famously said that he might have become a Christian, were it not for the Christians he had known. There is no shortage of examples of people who claimed to represent God yet lived in ways that desecrated and defamed the name of God. Priests abusing children, televangelists promising that God will enrich their viewers' lives if only they send an offering. But this also looks like the myriad ways in which ordinary people of faith don't practice what they preach.

But if it is true that we can profane God's name by our words and actions, we can also honor God's name by our words and actions. Most people become Christians because of a

Christian who demonstrated kindness, selfless love, just-
ness, and mercy—people who represented God well by their
words and actions. I am a Christian in part because my Roman
Catholic grandmother represented Jesus to me by her kindness and love in a way that drew me to God. And because of
the love shown me by a youth pastor and pastor of a small
church in my community when I was fourteen. I'm guessing
that as you reflect on your own journey, more than one person comes to mind who helped you become a person of faith.

Let's conclude this chapter by considering Jesus's approach
to keeping this commandment, not merely by avoiding profaning God's name but by positively hallowing God's name in
our words and in our deeds.

Representing God Well: Let Your Light Shine

Jesus's entire ministry was an effort to hallow God's name. His
efforts to heal the sick, welcome sinners, and feed the hungry
were all means of demonstrating God's presence among
human beings. He described his ministry as the "works I do
in my Father's name" (John 10:25) and said his purpose in life
was to reveal God's name to the world (John 17:6).

In Matthew, Jesus says, "Let your light shine before people, so they can see the good things you do and praise your
Father who is in heaven" (Matthew 5:16). To a similar end,
it's often been said that you are the only sermon some people
will hear, the only Bible some will read, and the only image
of God some will ever see.

We live in a time when fewer and fewer young adults,
Gen Z and millennials, are engaged in church. As I noted

above, many have been turned off by the hypocrisy they've seen from people in pews. For some, it feels like an older person's activity. Others find it boring and irrelevant. Many have some kind of faith—often identifying themselves as "spiritual but not religious." Most are repelled by any religion that feels like it is self-absorbed, narcissistic, judgmental, or mean-spirited.

As a pastor, I've had the joy of seeing many young adults return to church and become excited about their faith. They returned, in part, because they discovered a faith that spoke to both their intellect and their hearts. But from talking with many of them, I've come to see that they were most likely drawn by watching people of faith serve others selflessly through acts of compassion, justice, and mercy. And I see them doing the same in turn.

Recently I ate lunch at a restaurant near the church I serve. I was sitting alone, working on my weekend sermon. But midway through the meal, I overheard two young adults talking about the church. Not meaning to eavesdrop but unable to tune them out, I heard one tell his friend that he wasn't sure what he thought about attending a really big church, "but I love what they do for our community." The other spoke up, saying he'd heard about our work with low-income children through our partnerships with elementary schools across the city. He had also heard about our ministry to children, youth, and adults with special needs. He said, "If I was going to be a part of a church, it would be a church like that." These were two young people who didn't go to church, but they had been touched by our church's role in representing God's love to our community.

At one point in the Gospels, the disciples come to Jesus

and say to him, "Lord, teach us how to pray." In response, he gives them what we know as "the Our Father" or "the Lord's Prayer." In it, as I've alluded to above, Jesus teaches us to pray, "Hallowed be thy name." To hallow God's name is revere it or treat it as holy. It is the opposite of desecrating or profaning God's name. When I pray the Lord's Prayer, I ponder each line in my heart and often expand upon it in my own words. With regard to this line, I often say, "Lord, please use me to hallow your name. In my thoughts, in my words, and in my deeds, may I bring glory to your name."

At the peak of the coronavirus outbreak, I heard a story from a congregant named Bryan that was a powerful example of hallowing God's name with one's actions. One day, Bryan went to pick up a pizza at a local restaurant. His office is located near one of the most impoverished neighborhoods in Kansas City. He'd heard of a pizza place there and wanted to support its business, so he called in a carryout order. When he arrived, he saw there were a lot of children and youth waiting to pick up pizza. There were no parents to be seen.

Puzzled, he asked the owner, a man named Gary, what was up. He learned that for decades, word on the street had been that if a child's parents didn't feed them at night, Gary would provide them with a slice of pizza so they wouldn't go to bed hungry. Bryan was in awe. He paid for his pizza, and as he got ready to leave, Gary looked around at all these kids waiting for their free pizza, and he said with a smile, "Isn't God great?!"

Bryan told me, "I thought, here's a guy running a pizza place in one of the most underprivileged streets in the city during a global pandemic, and the only thing I could see on his face was pure joy. It was just awesome to see." No one expects a restaurant owner to give away food for free, but in doing so, this man became the vehicle by which God gave kids their daily bread.

This is what it looks like to hallow God's name. When we honor God's name in this way, we provide life to others, and we find life and joy in the process.

What Jesus Might Say to You

As my followers, you represent me. Just as I came to bring light to the world, and that light lives in you, I want you to let your light shine, that others might be drawn to, not repelled from, my Father because of you. You'll find joy and meaning and life as you seek to live each day in such a way that you hallow my name in your thoughts, words, and deeds.

IV

Rediscovering the Joy of Sabbath

Remember the Sabbath day and treat it as holy. Six days you may work and do all your tasks, but the seventh day is a Sabbath to Yahweh your God. Do not do any work on it—not you, your sons or daughters, your male or female servants, your animals, or the immigrant who is living with you. Because Yahweh made the heavens and the earth, the sea, and everything that is in them in six days, but rested on the seventh day. That is why Yahweh blessed the Sabbath day and made it holy.

—Exodus 20:8–11

On our thirtieth wedding anniversary, I planted a wild-flower garden for my wife, LaVon. It is about fifteen feet by fifty feet. In the middle of the plot, I erected a stone slab with the words "When I see wildflowers, I think of you" engraved upon it. The garden was meant to be an expression of my love for her.

Over the years, the weeds and grasses eventually took it over. So last year I killed all the overgrown foliage and re-seeded the soil. The flowers began to come up this year, but so did some weeds. I needed to spend some time in the flower garden cutting back the new weeds and the grasses, but I could never find the time. By the end of the summer, the garden had become an overgrown jungle again, with nearly all of the wildflowers choked out by the weeds.

One day, as I stood looking at this mess, a thought raced across my mind: "This is a metaphor for your life right now. You've crammed so much into your life, said yes to so many things you should have said no to. Your life is out of control, leaving you exhausted, with no time to tend the garden that is your soul."

Do you ever feel overcommitted, like there is no way you can get everything done? Do you feel like there are not enough hours in the day? Have you lost your joy in work you used to find joyful? Often think of quitting? Do you feel like you are physically or emotionally exhausted? In other words, do you ever wrestle with burnout?

For some of you, this is not a problem. You have a terrific "work-life balance." But a recent Gallup study of 7,500 full-time employees found that two-thirds of people feel burned out some of the time.[1] About a quarter report feeling burned out very often or always.

Concerning burnout, the bestselling author Brené Brown wrote,

> Here's a quote I once heard from a priest: "If you don't want to burn out, stop living like you're on fire." In to-

day's world, we are surrounded by a culture of scarcity that tells us we're not doing enough, that we don't have enough and that *we're* not enough, whether we're a stay-at-home parent or a CEO. . . . I've learned that I always have to be on the watch for burnout. Because when it creeps up on me, I don't like the person I become.[2]

I wonder if you've ever felt the same. Burnout can have serious consequences for our physical and mental health, our relationships, our job performance, and our spiritual lives.

I spoke with a pastor this week who told me there was a time when he had become so overcommitted he felt it was taking a toll on his marriage. He asked his wife, "Do you ever think about leaving me?" She said, "I've already divided the furniture in my head."

I've seen this, too, in so many of my congregation members. People who are burning the candle at both ends and have lost the joy in their lives. A couple recently told me that they were taking a weekend away, without children, leaving their work at home, for the first time since they began having children twelve years ago. They were excited but also emotionally and relationally exhausted.

Burnout—physical and emotional exhaustion—is correlated to depression and suicidal ideation. Among doctors, it is also correlated to increased medical errors. Medical errors result in approximately 250,000 deaths each year,[3] and those who report having made medical errors are more likely to also report burnout and fatigue.[4]

Entire books have been written on the causes, consequences, and cures of burnout. But long before it was a focus of scientific studies, and before government agencies began to explore the unintended consequences of workaholism and burnout, our Creator recognized our need for rest, renewal, and recreation—our need for Sabbath.

God's Concern for Workers

We live in a time when having at least one day off per week is assumed, and for many people, two days off is the norm. But when we look at the ancient world, there is no evidence that any nation or peoples observed a required day of rest until the advent of the Ten Commandments. Work was limited by the number of hours of daylight and was expected to take place every day.

Exodus 1:14 tells us about the working conditions of the Israelite slaves in Egypt. It says the Egyptians made the Israelites' lives "miserable with hard labor, making mortar and bricks, doing field work, and by forcing them to do all kinds of other cruel work." The Israelites groaned "because of their hard labor," the text reads (Exodus 2:23). Later, in Exodus 3:7, God says to Moses, "I've clearly *seen* my people oppressed in Egypt. I've *heard* their cry of injustice because of their slave masters. I *know* about their pain."

The story of God's liberation of the Israelites from Egypt begins with God's concern for the harsh working conditions they labored in. The insistence that the Israelites keep the Sabbath, and that they grant a Sabbath to their laborers and even their animals, was again a reflection of God's concern about quality of life, particularly for those who otherwise would not have a day of rest.

God's concern for workers is found throughout scripture. In Deuteronomy 24:14–15, we read:

> Don't take advantage of poor or needy workers, whether
> they are fellow Israelites or immigrants who live in your
> land or your cities. Pay them their salary the same day,
> before the sun sets, because they are poor, and their very
> life depends on that pay, and so they don't cry out against
> you to Yahweh. That would make you guilty.

Again and again in the Law of Moses and in the prophets,
scripture calls for not taking advantage of the poor. Farmers
were to leave the edges of their fields unharvested so the poor
and immigrants could harvest the leftover crops and eat.
Money and food were to be loaned to the poor without interest. Debts were forgiven every seventh year. In Deuteronomy 15:10, God says to the Israelites, "Give generously to
needy persons. Don't resent giving to them because it is this
very thing that will lead to Yahweh your God's blessing you
in all you do and work at."

In the New Testament, the apostle James offers these chal-
lenging words to those who enriched themselves while their
laborers struggled:

> Listen! Hear the cries of the wages of your field hands.
> These are the wages you stole from those who harvested
> your fields. The cries of the harvesters have reached the
> ears of the Lord of heavenly forces. You have lived a self-
> satisfying life on this earth, a life of luxury. You have
> stuffed your hearts in preparation for the day of slaughter.
> (James 5:4–5)

These and many other passages remind us that there can be no
question about God's concern for the poor and the powerless.

The question for us is how these concerns should be addressed today, in a free-market economy. Is the honoring of God's concern for workers and the poor the job only of the individual? Or does society, through the making of just rules and regulations, play some part in protecting the vulnerable?

Here I'm reminded of Harvard professor Harvey Cox and his recent book, *The Market as God*.[5] Cox argues that the market itself has become a modern deity, a golden calf, in whom many of us have put our deepest trust. By its providential care, it is said, all of these concerns will be resolved. As industry gets more efficient and profitable, even the poorest among us will see their buying power rise. The free market does work in mysterious ways, and I do think it is a better economic plan than many alternatives. But the market has no conscience, no sense of right and wrong, no compassion or kindness. Humans must inject these things into the system.

Which leads us back to the fourth commandment.

Our creator recognized our innate need for rest, renewal, and recreation. These were important for human flourishing. So to the former slaves, only recently liberated from their oppressive working conditions, God said:

Remember the Sabbath day and treat it as holy. Six days you may work and do all your tasks, but the seventh day is a Sabbath to Yahweh your God. Do not do any work on it—not you, your sons or daughters, your male or female servants, your animals, or the immigrant who is living with you. (Exodus 20:8–10)

For the first time in history, a nation's God proclaimed a universal day of rest. It was *not* a good economic decision. It represented the instant loss of 14 percent of labor, commerce, and production, as people and livestock stopped producing for one day in seven. But despite the economic loss, it represented an important leap forward for helping human beings to experience the good life. The idea was so compelling that other religions eventually embraced it. Nations and governments accepted it too.

The Sabbath is the gift of a loving God who cares for his people, who wishes for them a good and beautiful life. So let's take an even deeper look at this command.

Remember the Sabbath

The fourth commandment begins, "Remember the Sabbath." In the Hebrew Bible, when God remembers someone, it usually means that God is mindful of that person and will act on their behalf. Remembering is not a casual thing. It means keeping something front of mind as an expression of its importance. For example, at the Last Supper, Jesus tells the disciples to repeat the meal of bread and wine and to do this "in remembrance of me" (Luke 22:19).

The act of remembering is a way of signaling the importance of that which is being remembered. In Exodus 20, we read the theological foundation for remembering the Sabbath: *Because Yahweh made the heavens and the earth, the sea, and everything that is in them in six days, but rested on the seventh day. That is why Yahweh blessed the Sabbath day and made it holy.*

Did God need to rest? No, but the verse makes clear that neither is God a workaholic. There is a time for resting and reflecting, even for God himself. God established this sacred rhythm and modeled it *for us*. The Sabbath was a day for God to stop and take in all the beauty of a creation he himself declared to be "very good."

Among my many faults, one is that I seldom stop for long to celebrate the wonderful and blessed things that happen in my life. When good things happen in my family or in the church I serve, I'm always thinking about what is next; what needs to be done now and tomorrow and the next day. I don't savor the victories for long, if at all. I'm lousy at stopping to smell the roses. *But this way of living misses so many blessings.* It lacks the space for gratitude and rejoicing, and it can be exhausting to go from one thing straight to the next. Sabbath is about *stopping to savor, to enjoy, to reflect, to be in awe, to celebrate, to give thanks, and to be renewed.*

In Deuteronomy 5, we find the Ten Commandments repeated. The chapter is set forty years after the commandments' unveiling, as Moses nears death and the children of Israel prepare to enter the Promised Land. The versions of the commandments in Exodus and Deuteronomy are virtually identical, but there are two differences in the command concerning the Sabbath. In Exodus, the fourth commandment says to *remember* the Sabbath. Deuteronomy says to *keep* the Sabbath. And the rationale for keeping the commandment is different as well.

In Exodus, the rationale for Sabbath-keeping is tied to God's resting after creation. We are, in turn, invited to rest, celebrate the goodness of creation, and in doing so be renewed. In Deuteronomy, the rationale for the Sabbath is to remember the Exodus and God's deliverance of Israel: "Remember that you were a slave in Egypt, but Yahweh your God brought you out of there with a strong hand and an outstretched arm. That's why Yahweh your God commands you to keep the Sabbath day" (Deuteronomy 5:15).

In essence, in Deuteronomy the Sabbath is a day for God's people to remember what he did for them and to give thanks for it. They are to keep the Sabbath and, as they do, to remember and give thanks for God's love, mercy, and compassion shown in his deliverance of the Israelites from slavery in Egypt.

In both cases the Sabbath is not just about resting. It is about remembering, reflecting, celebrating *God's* work in creating the world with all of its blessings, and pondering God's deliverance and our identity as his people.

Treat It as Holy

The command goes on to tell us that we are to treat the Sabbath as holy. The word "holy" here is the Hebrew word *qadash*. It usually means something is set apart for God. Again we learn that the Sabbath was not only about rest. To set it apart as holy means treating it as a day given to God. While our entire lives belong to God, God has claimed one day in seven as being specifically his.

Jews observe the Sabbath from Friday at sunset to Saturday at sunset. That's because the Jewish day begins at sunset, following a pattern established in the creation story of Genesis 1:5 (NRSV), where we read, "God called the light 'day,' and the darkness he called 'night.' And there was evening, and there was morning—the first day." This refrain is repeated throughout the creation story, leading Jews to count days as starting at sunset.

Early in the church's history, Christians gathered to worship on Sunday, the "first day of the week," because it was on that day that Jesus rose from the dead. For us, Sabbath celebrates not only God's work in creating the earth but also God's redemptive work in Jesus's crucifixion and resurrection. Every Sabbath is meant to be a celebration of Easter and Christ's triumph over evil, hate, sin, and death.

But just as we've done with the name of God, we have done with the day that God claims as his own. We have profaned it.

There was a time when committed churchgoers attended worship every weekend unless they were sick. But today our travel schedules, our workloads, our kids' soccer schedules, our golf and recreation schedules all leave little room for pausing to pray, celebrating God's blessings, reflecting upon scripture, and joining together with other Christians to "grow in the grace and knowledge of our Lord and savior" (2 Peter 3:18). We have taken a day intended to be holy, and we have made it ordinary. Even when we do take time to rest, reflect, and recreate, we often leave God out of our Sabbath observance.

In the chapter on the first commandment, we learned about our tendency to edge God out. Observance of the Sabbath is another area where we do this.

What has happened to our day of rest that was set apart as holy? We've overprogrammed it, along with the rest of our lives, so that we don't have an hour to worship, pray, commune with other Christians, and feast at the Lord's table. We're too *busy*.

One thing I've learned from my friend Rabbi Art Nemitoff is the idea of planning one's entire week around the Sabbath. This practice is central to Judaism. Observant Jewish families long for the Sabbath all week. They look forward to it. They order their lives around it. As the sunset approaches on the Sabbath—the Shabbat—they have already prepared for the day. It is a day holy to the Lord.

Several years ago, I was able to enjoy a Shabbat dinner with the Nemitoff family. They gathered their children and a handful of friends and shared a beautiful meal that began with a blessing giving thanks to God, "who brings forth bread from the earth." This was followed by meaningful conversations about life and faith. I left that night thinking, "I want my Sabbath celebration to be more like that!"

Counting the Cost

The commandment continues:

> Six days you may work and do all your tasks, but the seventh day is a Sabbath to Yahweh your God. Do not do any work on it—not you, your sons or daughters, your male or female servants, your animals, or the immigrant who is living with you. (Exodus 20:9–10)

The Sabbath was not just for the wealthy but also for the poor. It was not just for the parents but also for the children. It was not only for the Israelites but also for the immigrants in their midst. And it was not just for people but even for the animals (and the fields, and the fruit-bearing trees, and all of creation). The Sabbath was God's response to our relentless pursuit of hurry, busy, going, doing. God knew we needed this.

Listen to what God says about the commandment in Exodus 31:13–14:

> Tell the Israelites: "Be sure to keep my sabbaths, because the Sabbath is a sign between me and you in every generation so you will know that I am Yahweh who makes you holy. Keep the Sabbath, because it is holy for you. Everyone who violates the Sabbath will be put to death."

It is surprising to find that the death penalty was prescribed for violating the Sabbath. (In fact, it's one of the very things that caused Richard Dawkins to take issue with the Ten Commandments in the article I cited earlier.) Why such a harsh penalty? At minimum, it seems intended to make clear that God was serious about observing the Sabbath. God knew there would always be commerce to transact, money to be made, work to be done, and his people would be tempted to pursue these on the Sabbath. But God said, "No, not on this day. You are to rest, to give your employees rest, your children rest, your animals rest."

I also wonder if the death penalty was a metaphor, a way of pointing to the impact of not resting: If you are unwilling to stop and rest, your health will deteriorate, your relationships will suffer, and in a thousand other ways you will pay the price. If you die of a heart attack at age fifty-five because you seldom took time to rest and reduce your stress, or if you end up divorced because you never made time to rest, renew, and play with your family, was it worth it? Failing to observe the Sabbath results in a kind of death penalty for each of us: exhaustion coupled with the loss of joy, of relationships, of gratitude, and of so many of the things that are meant to enrich our lives.

Debates About the Sabbath

So the Sabbath is a gift, and it is a rule to live by. But the challenge of rules, even good ones, is that we can get so focused on the rule that we end up missing its intent.

When we're told not to work on the Sabbath, we naturally want to know, "Okay, so what constitutes work? Are we allowed to cook? To clean? Can we mow the yard?" By the time of Jesus, the teachers of the Law had spent a great deal of time studying what constituted work and therefore could not be done on the Sabbath. Eventually a list of thirty-nine categories of forbidden activities was developed. Here are a few examples of activities that are forbidden on the Sabbath, based upon the prohibitions found in the Talmud:

- Adding fresh water to a vase of cut flowers (for this is a form of sowing)
- Separating good fruit from spoiled fruit (for this is a form of harvesting)
- Cutting hair or nails (for this is like shearing your animals)
- Braiding hair (for this is like weaving)
- Rubbing soap to make lather (for this is like scraping animals' skins)
- Switching off an electric light (for this is like extinguishing a fire)

Visitors to Israel are often struck by the fact that on the Sabbath, the elevators at their hotel are programmed to stop on each floor automatically. It's inconvenient if you're going to the top floor, but it keeps you from needing to push the button of your floor, which is considered work.

These detailed prohibitions related to the Sabbath are referenced throughout the Gospels, creating a clear tension between Jesus and the religious leaders of his day. This tension sprang from the very different way in which Jesus interpreted and applied the Law.

In Mark, Jesus's first act of public ministry occurred on a Sabbath, when he entered the synagogue and began to teach. As he was teaching, a person with an evil spirit began to scream, and Jesus cast out the evil spirit (Mark 1:21–25). It was the first of many times he healed on the Sabbath—an act that was prohibited except in life-or-death situations.

Matthew 12:9–14 is another great example:

Jesus left that place and went into their synagogue. A man with a withered hand was there. Wanting to bring charges against Jesus, [the religious leaders] asked, "Does the Law allow a person to heal on the Sabbath?" Jesus replied, "Who among you has a sheep that falls into a pit on the Sabbath and will not take hold of it and pull it out? How much more valuable is a person than a sheep! So the Law allows a person to do what is good on the Sabbath." Then Jesus said to the man, "Stretch out your hand." So he did and it was made healthy, just like the other one. The Pharisees went out and met in order to find a way to destroy Jesus.

For those who were teasing out rule after rule of what constituted violations of the Sabbath, Jesus's interpretation of the command must have been very frustrating. Others found it liberating. In explaining his view, he said, "The Sabbath was created for humans; humans weren't created for the Sabbath" (Mark 2:27).

Notice, however, that Jesus doesn't say, "The Sabbath is not important" or "You don't have to observe the Sabbath." Jesus removes the nitpicking over definitions, but he never sets aside the Sabbath itself. The Sabbath is clearly important to Jesus. He routinely enters the synagogue on the Sabbath. He ministers and teaches on the Sabbath. He helps others on the Sabbath. And presumably, he rests and renews with his disciples on the Sabbath. Jesus moves from a Sabbath observance built around rules to one built around people. This included rest and renewal, and for Jesus, it seems also to have included gathering for prayer in the synagogue. He saw that the intent of the Sabbath was to bless God's people, and he spent his Sabbaths doing just that.

Reclaiming the Sabbath

Of all the remaining commandments in this book, this is the one that most convicts me today. To be clear, the commandment enjoining us to honor parents and the ones forbidding murder, adultery, stealing, bearing false witness, and coveting all mean more than meets the eye. As we will see, they have much to teach us when read through the eyes of Jesus. But it is the command to Sabbath that speaks to the emotional, spiritual, and physical exhaustion many of us feel. It is the command I've felt most challenged and encouraged by.

My kids had hamsters when they were growing up. Have you ever watched a hamster on a hamster wheel? Their eyes are focused straight ahead, and they run faster and faster. I wonder what it is they imagine they're running toward, what it is that motivates these cute little animals to strain themselves as they do.

They are a perfect metaphor for where many of us find ourselves. We get on the hamster wheel and we run. We're not even sure what the end goal is anymore, but we run. We are weary and exhausted, but we keep running.

I have a terrible habit of saying yes to things, and a very hard time saying no. Recently I was asked to attend a meeting in another city. I flew there and spent two days participating in this gathering—a gathering that I knew before committing to it did not really require my presence. The people at that meeting could handle what they were doing without me. But I loved the people and didn't want to say no, so I rearranged my schedule and added no small bit of stress. (My regular work still needed to be done, only now it would be done late into the night.) When I boarded the airplane home, I thought, "This meeting would have ended with the exact same results whether I had been there or not."

My daughter and son-in-law run a fresh-cut-flower and vegetable stand at the farmers' market in Lawrence, Kansas, about forty-five minutes from my home. It is held on Saturday mornings, which are usually when I get caught up on work and complete the final revisions to my sermon in preparation for the first of our weekend services, Saturday night at five. Recently my daughter said to me, "Dad, did you know JT and I have been running our stand at the farmers' market for four years now, and you've never been to see it?" I could tell she was disappointed—she had every right to be—and had been holding this inside for some time.

Being a dad is one of the most important things in the world to me, and I desperately want to be a good one. I apologized to her profusely. "I'll be there next weekend," I said.

All week it ate at me. The next weekend, I rearranged my schedule and was there with her. It required saying no to some things, but in doing so, I was saying yes to things that were more important. My presence said to my daughter that I heard her, I cared about her and her husband, and they mattered more to me than my work.

I'm sharing this story because my hunch is that some of you reading this book are, like me, overcommitted people who have a hard time saying no. And often it is your health, your family, and your faith that suffer for it. I think God wants to say to those who struggle with this, "Remember the Sabbath and keep it holy." We should work hard during the week and give our best. But one day in seven, we're meant to get off the hamster wheel.

Recently I read Mark Buchanan's excellent book *The Rest of God*. He notes, "The root idea of Sabbath is simple as rain falling, basic as breathing. It's that all living things thrive only by an ample measure of stillness."[6] I heard many people say something similar during the shelter-in-place orders imposed during the novel coronavirus pandemic. While fear, anxiety, and uncertainty were in the air, there was this remarkable sense I heard again and again from members of my congregation that a silver lining was the time they were spending at home, eating meals around the dinner table, reading, playing games as a family, taking walks. No one wanted the pandemic to continue, but I heard many people express their hope that the newfound rest they experienced, and the relinquishing of hurry's control in their lives, might become a new normal for them.

God takes delight when you show up for worship on the Sabbath, when you pause to remember who you are and whose you are. And God loves to see you play with your children. It is *not* wasted time. It is part of what you were made for. God wants you to have dinner with your friends, to hold your spouse, to sit on a porch swing and read a good book. And God is pleased when you take some time alone to think, pray, and read.

I want to ask you to do something right now, here in the margin of this book: Write down four things that renew you—that bring you joy—that you may not have done in a while. Or maybe they are things that you know you haven't done enough of lately.

What if you turned off the television, social media, said no to work on the Sabbath? What if, instead, you used this day as if it were holy to God, revering him in worship, and then did these things that renew you—*this next Sabbath*? And what if you committed to remembering the Sabbath and keeping it holy with greater intentionality from this time on? How would it impact your life?

I can tell you how: If you remember the Sabbath and keep it holy, your faith will grow deeper, your stress will be lowered, your mental health will be improved, and your workweek may even be more productive. If you are married, your marriage will be stronger. If you have kids, your relationship with them will be better. All if you would simply (say it out loud) *remember the Sabbath and keep it holy*.

What Jesus Might Say to You

I see how hard you work, how many things you do, how weary and tired you often feel. I long to give you rest, to see you recreate and be renewed. My Father gave the Sabbath as a gift for you. You need it. It is not optional. But only you can decide to make this a part of your life. You must also know that he considers the Sabbath his day, a day when he longs for you to honor him with your presence, your prayers, and your worship. Remember the Sabbath and keep it as holy, and you will find that the Sabbath will bless you.

THE SECOND TABLET

The Call to Love One's Neighbor

You must love your neighbor as yourself; I am Yahweh.

—Leviticus 19:18

V

A Question of Honor

Honor your father and your mother so that your
life will be long on the fertile land that Yahweh
your God is giving you.

—Exodus 20:12

Whenever I teach or preach on the fifth commandment,
the command to honor our parents, people raise ob-
jections. What if your parents were not honorable? What if
they were abusive? Do you still have to honor them? Tragically, there are many people who were harmed sexually, physically, or emotionally by their parents. Others simply had a
very poor relationship with the people who raised them. Either way, their relationship with their parents has brought
them great pain.

My parents weren't abusive, but caring, yet when I was a
teenager, I chafed under this commandment too. Especially
when honoring my parents seemed to mean obeying rules
that felt unjust (or, as I may have said then, "stupid"!). But as

we'll see, this command in its historical context was about so much more than submitting to the authority of a parent, whether or not that parent was loving toward their child. It was about how each generation had a call to care for those who had come before them.

In our mid-fifties, LaVon and I have the joy of being parents to our daughters (and son-in-law) and grandparents to a granddaughter who just turned six as I was completing this manuscript. Even though our daughters are in their early thirties, we look for ways to regularly express our support and care for them. We encourage them, cheer them on, and give wise counsel if asked. But it's also been a joy to watch them expressing care for us, checking in on us, encouraging us, and seeking to give us counsel.

As our children's need for our support has declined, we've found the needs of our own parents ramping up. There was special care given to LaVon's dad in the last year of his life. We've had trips with our moms to the emergency room, six surgeries, and a move from home to assisted living for one of them. There have been bills to pay, doctors' visits, preparing homes for sale, and lots of reassurance and encouragement. And this kind of care is, in large part, what scholars believe the fifth commandment was meant to address.

Literature from the ancient Near East, from Mesopotamia to Egypt, makes it clear that people were expected to care for their aging parents. I'm not aware of another specific commandment to "honor your parents," but Mesopotamian texts mention the need to provide parents with oil, grain, and wool—in essence, food and clothing—as these were considered essential for life. There are a host of other texts documenting provisions that were made for parents and those without children. If a person was childless, they could adopt adult children, giving them a share of their estate as an inheritance in exchange for the promise of care for the adopted parent in old age. A son who did not support his aging parents was forbidden from receiving his inheritance upon their death.[1]

To the Israelites, who were preparing to form a new nation, the command to "honor your father and your mother" was so important, so foundational for creating a good society, that it appeared first among all of the commandments related to how we live in relationship with others. And as we will see, it continues to be important, not only for parents and children of all ages but also for the broader concern a society is meant to have for its older adults.

Exceptions to Rules: When Parents Act Dishonorably

The federal Administration for Children & Families estimated that in 2017, 674,000 children were victims of maltreatment. In total, 74.9 percent of victims were neglected, 18.3 percent were physically abused, and 8.6 percent were sexually abused.[2] And 1,720 children died from maltreatment by their parents that year.

What do the authors of scripture say about those parents? Do we honor them? No, we don't honor abusers. In fact, I don't think the fifth commandment is written to address abusive parents or neglectful and harmful people. They are the exception to this rule.

When we set boundaries as adults in how we will relate to parents who were unloving, or when law enforcement removes children from abusive homes, it is not a violation of the fifth commandment but a recognition that abusive or neglectful parents are no longer acting as legitimate parents. Let me be clear: *The command to honor our parents is not a requirement to continue to be abused by someone who acts in ways that are inconsistent with a legitimate and loving parent.*

If you were abused, neglected, or otherwise hurt by your parents, there are other precepts in scripture you might turn to, and there are therapists specializing in abuse or neglect who can help you find healing. Your pastor might also be of help as you consider the theological questions and seek to find healing in your faith.

Part of that healing may come in practicing Jesus's call: "Love your enemies. Do good to those who hate you. Bless those who curse you. Pray for those who mistreat you" (Luke 6:27–28). The love Jesus speaks about in this passage is not affection or an ongoing relationship. It does not mean excusing the inexcusable or saying the abuse or neglect did not matter. It is a spiritual exercise that often allows the one harmed to rise above the pain and find release. It often increases the likelihood of forgiveness—which, I'll repeat, is not excusing the inexcusable but choosing to release the bitterness and pain so that the abuser can no longer have power over you.

Recognizing, then, that there are exceptions to the rule to honor our parents, and that your family situation might be an exception, let's move on to explore the command as it applies to most people—the call to honor our father and our mother.

What Does It Mean to Honor?

Let's begin by unpacking what it means to *honor* one's father and mother. The Hebrew word for honor is *kavad* (or *kaved* or *kavod*), which means "heavy" or "weighty"—or, as a verb, to consider or treat as weighty. The opposite of heavy, in Hebrew, is *qalah,* which means "light" and is used as a verb to signify disrespect—to take something or someone lightly, to trivialize or to neglect or to ignore them. We treat our parents as weighty when we take seriously their values and needs and experience. Or we can take them lightly, trivializing them as if their needs or opinions carry no weight with us.

When we're young and our parents are seeking to protect us or teach us, to consider them "weighty" includes obedience. Paul makes this clear in Ephesians 6:1: "As for children," he writes, "obey your parents in the Lord, because it is right." He then goes on to cite the command to honor one's parents. Interestingly, the Hebrew word usually translated as "obey" is *shema,* which generally means "to hear" or "to listen." In this sense, honoring one's parents would mean to listen to them, to hear their words and concerns.

The older we get, the less our parents should demand obedience. What they rightly hope for is to be heard. If I know my mother or father wants me to do something, I will take it seriously, because they are my parents, and I consider their wants, needs, and desires important. But I may need to tell them that I cannot do what they've asked. As a child, this usually would have been inappropriate. But as an adult, my other obligations—to my wife, my children, my job, and my faith—may require me to say no to the wishes of a parent. I have known parents who sought to exert undue influence over their adult children's choice of mates, careers, and other life decisions, or who had unfair expectations regarding anything from which holidays were "theirs" to how frequently their children were supposed to call or visit. In situations like these, hearing one's parent might not be the same as obeying their request.

But even when we can't obey our parents, honoring them means that we refrain from belittling them, abusing them, cursing them, speaking ill of them, or harming them. In fact, these kinds of violations of the command were taken very seriously in the Law. They could lead to the death penalty for children who cursed their parents or persistently did what was evil to them.[3] I've known people who always seemed to speak ill of their parents when their parents came up in conversation. In general, it's a good idea to refrain from saying something about a person when they are not present that you wouldn't say about them if they were present.

My mom and I butted heads a lot when I was in high school. I loved her, yet she drove me crazy. (I expect that my mom will read this book, so I know I'm not violating the rule I laid out in the last paragraph!) I also know that during that time, I drove her crazy too. During the teenage years, we are self-differentiating, questioning authority, yearning for freedom. We see things from our own perspective so clearly while often struggling to see things from our parents' perspective. Their rules can seem stifling and even absurd. I felt these things intensely, and it came out in the way I treated my mom.

At times, I got in trouble because I hadn't finished my chores around the house, or because I came home after curfew (and why did I need a curfew anyway?). Once, my mom didn't want me to travel out of town with kids in my youth group, led by our pastor, for a Bible quiz tournament. "Mom, really?" I remember saying. "I can't go out of town for a *Bible quiz tournament*???" She did end up letting me go to the Bible quiz tournament, but it really upset her and ended in a huge argument. Years later, she told me she'd had a vision of me dying in a car accident and was afraid to lose me. Only then could I see the irony that I was arguing and fighting with my mom *about going to compete in a Bible quiz tournament*. While I had memorized whole sections of scripture, my impatience with my mother was a sign that I was not living one of the Ten Commandments.

I had become a Christian at fourteen years old. In those years, I was reading scripture and trying very hard to apply it to my life—to live the words I was reading. I found that I could treat complete strangers with love. I could be patient and kind to classmates, to kids in my youth group, and even to other adults. But at times, it seemed much harder to act the same way with my mom. I was perpetually frustrated with her attempts to control me.

What I could not see at that time were the challenges my mom was facing. For years, she had worked as a real estate agent. During my junior year of high school, when interest rates hit their historic high of 18 percent, the real estate market crashed. My stepdad worked as a home builder, and they lost everything. An alcoholic, he addressed the financial pain by drinking—and when he drank, he became angry and sometimes violent. Our family's life was unraveling. But at sixteen, while I knew about my stepdad's alcoholism, I didn't understand all of the turmoil my mom was navigating at work. She kept that from me. All I could see was how unreasonable and controlling I thought she was being.

That was thirty-eight years ago. In the years since, I've apologized and sought to make it up to my mom, but I still regret my angry words as I chafed under her rules. In the end we survived my teenage years, she eventually divorced, and we have a good relationship today. My mom is one of my heroes. I am grateful for the grace she showed me then and now.

Speaking Your Parents' Love Language

When we're little, we tend to only take from our parents. We need food, shelter, clothing, protection, and love. But the fifth commandment tells us that we're not meant only to take; we are also responsible to care for our parents.

As we grow and mature, we begin to see our parents as human beings. We recognize that they are not invincible. They have needs. They get hurt. They have feelings. They not only give love but also need love. One sign of emotional and spiritual maturity is thinking of the needs of others before our own. When we're little, that shows up in the love we share with our parents—the hugs and notes and expressions of care that children seem to naturally offer their parents from a very early age. We sometimes forget these, however, as we enter the teen years.

Honoring—treating someone as weighty, important, significant—includes considering their needs, their feelings, and what might bless them. I wonder, how well do you know your parents' likes, interests, and desires?

Gary Chapman's classic book, *The Five Love Languages,* was written to help couples understand how to give love in the way that their mate best hears love. His premise is that there are five primary ways that people receive or experience love:

- words of affirmation
- acts of service
- receiving gifts
- quality time
- physical touch

We tend to speak the love language—that is, to give love in the way—that's meaningful to us, but it might not always be the way those closest to us best receive or hear love. This idea has had a significant impact on my marriage as I came to know and speak my wife's love language.

While Chapman initially wrote his book to help couples, I believe the same idea can apply to parents and children.[4] An effective parent will learn their child's primary love language so that their child experiences love. The same applies if you're a child trying to find ways to honor and care for your parent.

You can find Chapman's tests online to help you discover your love language. It might be fun for you to have your parents take the test as well, and for you to discuss one another's love languages together. LaVon and I have done this with our children in the past, discussing their love languages and our own. But as I write these words, I realize that I have never asked my parents to take the test, and never really thought about their love language. It may be time for my parents to take the test. I also realize that it would be good to do this again with our now-grown children. I think I know their love languages, and they mine, but I'm not sure.

My primary love language is words of affirmation, with physical touch and quality time as close seconds. Recently, one of my daughters sent me a text that said, "Hey, just thinking of you today. I'm so proud to call you my dad and am constantly impressed by how hard you work and how much you care for people. I love you, Dad." That text really touched me and made me feel loved. She was speaking my primary love language.

What are your parents' love languages? What is yours? Have you honored them lately by speaking your love for them in a way they can hear?

The Primary Meaning of Honor? Caring for the Aging

Many scholars believe that the fifth commandment's primary intent was to ensure people cared for the elderly. Throughout most of human history, programs like Social Security, Medicare, and pension plans did not exist. There were no independent-living or assisted-living homes. What did exist was the social covenant spelled out in the fifth commandment. Younger generations were meant to care for the needs of older generations, and it was understood that this happened, primarily, through the family.

Until the 1900s, families lived together in multigenerational homes or adjacent to one another. Most people worked until their bodies forced them to slow down or stop. By this time, adult children were helping to carry the load for their parents while teaching their own children to help. Honoring one's parents—considering them weighty, important, paying attention to them—meant caring for them as they grew older.

The Great Depression played a big part in changing how we lived out this commandment. When the economy crashed, massive numbers of senior adults could no longer provide for their own needs, nor could their families or communities support them. Congress passed the Social Security Act of 1935 to address these vulnerable populations, providing a regular source of income for the disabled and those in "old age."[5] Social Security has been a lifesaver for many people since its inception.

But today the Social Security Administration suggests that most people will be unable to live in retirement solely on their Social Security retirement benefit. (In 2019 the average payout was $17,640 per year.) Retirees will need to draw from pensions, savings, and investments, the Social Security Administration suggests, in order to make ends meet. But fewer companies offer a pension today, and many baby boomers have saved very little for retirement. Forty-five percent of boomers, according to one study, have less than $25,000 in retirement savings.[6]

It seems likely that Gen Xers and millennials will need to help their baby-boomer parents financially as their parents age. This may mean a return to the practice of multiple generations living together and sharing household expenses, or it might mean other forms of economic assistance. It may seem a burden to many, but it is how most human beings have lived throughout history, and it was likely what God intended when he instructed the Israelites to honor their fathers and mothers.

Most of my closest friends are in the same life phase as LaVon and me. Their parents are in their seventies and eighties, and some of them have saved very little for retirement. Two of my good friends have parents who either are in the hospital as I write this chapter or were just released. Several have lost parents in the last few years.

Recently, a group of us sat at dinner talking about our parents and the care we're all seeking to extend to them. One of our friends said, "Let's not forget this as we grow older." They were referring specifically to the difficult conversation one of them was having with a parent about not driving anymore. This elder parent was determined to go out on his own, even though his driving skills were compromised. He became agitated when his kids suggested giving up the car. My friend dropped the conversation, and then one day the parent got into an accident that could have seriously hurt someone. We each said, "Let's not make our kids have this conversation with us."

There are a host of decisions we can make as we age that will help our children honor us and avoid creating frustration. We've also talked about the importance of simplifying our lives, of giving away what we don't need instead of leaving things for our kids to sort through, and of making sure we have living wills that are fair to all our children. I've watched poorly designed estate plans create conflict among siblings after a parent has died.

As a parent of adult children and a son of aging parents, I've come to see that all of us have a role in upholding this command—even parents. We want to bless our children, encourage them, and make it as easy as possible for them to honor us in our later years. If you're midlife or beyond, have you done all you need to do to make it easier for your children to honor you as you grow older?

Jesus, Honoring Parents, and Caring for Elder Orphans

In the Gospels, Jesus directly quotes this commandment on two occasions. The first is a brief reference in Matthew 19, when Jesus speaks to the "rich young ruler" and cites the fifth commandment as one of the keys to inheriting eternal life.

The second mention is more substantial. It comes in Mark 7, when Jesus challenges a tradition or legal judgment of the Pharisees. They had apparently determined (though this ruling would be changed in later Judaism) that if a son was angry with his parents, he could say, "Whatever I might have used to help you I'm now dedicating to God." In other words, if the man was dedicating some indeterminate portion of his resources to the temple in Jerusalem, he would no longer be obliged, or even allowed, to use these resources to help his parents. It was considered a sacred vow that could not be rescinded, even if the parents were later to need the son's help.

In short, the Pharisees taught that the vow dedicating the son's resources to God and the temple had greater binding authority than the fifth commandment. But listen to Jesus's response to this tradition or ruling:

> Moses said, *Honor your father and your mother,* and *The person who speaks against father or mother will certainly be put to death.* But you say, "If you tell your father or mother, 'Everything I'm expected to contribute to you is *corban* (that is, a gift I'm giving to God),' then you are no longer required to care for your father or mother." In this way you do away with God's word in favor of the rules handed down to you, which you pass on to others. (Mark 7:10–13)

Vows are important, particularly religious ones. But Jesus makes clear that they are not more important than the obligation to honor your parents. Further, this passage makes clear that Jesus saw a connection between honoring one's parents and providing financial support to them.

LaVon and I have always given the first 10 percent of our income to God and God's work through the church. As our income grew over the years, we began giving an increasing percentage of our income away, above our tithe, largely to programs and ministries working with children and adults in poverty. But the fifth commandment and Jesus's comments about it in Mark 7 have always served as an important reminder to us that God expects us to care for our parents should they need our support.

Of course, honoring our aging parents is not just about helping them financially. For many reading this book, your aging parents will never need your financial help. But they *will* need your touch, your friendship, your counsel. They will need you to help them feel valued, respected, worthy—in other words, to help them feel honored. In Romans 13:8 Paul writes, "Don't be in debt to anyone, except for the obligation to love each other."

As we consider this nuance of the fifth commandment, it is interesting to consider Jesus's relationship with his own mother. She seems to have traveled with him and participated actively in his ministry. According to John, Jesus performed his first miracle (or "sign," as John calls it) at a wedding reception in Cana of Galilee. When the wine ran out, Mary came to her son and asked if he could help. It seems likely she hoped he might go and purchase more wine. Jesus responds, rather cryptically—as is common in the Gospel of John— "Woman, what does that have to do with me? My time hasn't come yet" (John 2:4). Nevertheless, *because his mother asked,* he performs his first miracle, transforming water into wine. He did not plan to do this miraculous sign at this time, but he honors his mother by doing what she asks.

Jesus is modeling something important for us here. There are times when our parents ask something of us, and we don't really have the time or inclination to do it, yet honoring our parents may mean making the time and doing what they asked. This is a form of honoring your parents. (This is not to say that we must always do what they ask us as adults, as noted earlier in the chapter.)

But the most remarkable scene involving Jesus and the fifth commandment takes place as he hangs dying on the cross. The scene, described in John 19:25–27, is deeply moving:

> Jesus' mother and his mother's sister, Mary the wife of Clopas, and Mary Magdalene stood near the cross. When Jesus saw his mother and the disciple whom he loved standing nearby, he said to his mother, "Woman, here is your son." Then he said to the disciple, "Here is your mother." And from that time on, this disciple took her into his home.

The "disciple whom Jesus loved" is believed to be John. Jesus looks upon his mother from the cross and expresses concern for her. He wants to make sure she is cared for after his death. He hangs there in torment, yet his concern is for his mother.[7]

Jesus called John to care for Mary. To honor her *as if she were John's own mother.* I wonder if there are people whom Christ is calling you to honor—to care for—because they have no one else to care for them? In thirty-five years of ministry, I have visited with many senior adults who did not have family of their own, and my life has always been enriched by these encounters. They teach, encourage, and bless me.

Today, about 22 percent of older adults fall into a category demographers call "elder orphans." They have no children, or at least none living in the town where they live, and their spouse has died. Seventy percent of these seniors have no designated caregiver in the event that they become disabled or ill.[8] These persons will need all the things parents need from their children, but either they don't have children or their children are not involved in their lives.

Many do fine. They have friends and other relationships that sustain them, people who come alongside them, and other resources that support their needs. Church is a huge part of this. But I wonder if the fifth commandment, seen through the lens of Jesus's call for his disciple John to care for Mary, might be a call to all of us not only to care for our *own* parents but also to care for older adults in our communities. These older adults may be your neighbors, your coworkers, your aunts and uncles, or people in your church. They could also be people you've never met before who live in some kind of senior housing but have no children who come to visit.

Years ago, one of our church's members, Karla Woodward, told me that she had a vision for a ministry for senior adults in retirement communities, and particularly for those in assisted-living centers. Our church had been visiting area nursing homes for some time, but she wanted to expand this and get more people involved. Today the ministry, called SilverLink, visits more than thirty care centers a month, holding worship services for the residents. We also have a ministry where members bring their dogs and cats to visit the elderly who live in care centers where residents are not allowed to have their own pets living with them. It is amazing to watch how the residents, particularly those who always loved pets, come alive when a cat or dog comes for a visit. Some families take their children and grandchildren to visit senior adults who never get to see their own grandchildren but who have, in essence, been adopted by these grandchildren. Other church members hold a monthly worship service in our chapel for people with Alzheimer's and dementia. A dozen skilled-care centers bring their residents to our campus. Some of them no longer remember their own names, but as we sing old familiar hymns, they sing and smile and sense the love of God through our volunteers.

One of our members recently described a visit with an elderly man. Our member listened as the man shared stories from his life and the wisdom he'd gained through it all. The congregant was moved by the experience of hearing this man's stories. He shared a scripture and then prayed for the man he'd come to visit. As he prepared to leave, the older man said to him, "I think this is so important, your coming to visit me. It means a lot to me. Really, more than you can know. When I was a young man, I did the same—I visited the elderly and loved it. And now you are visiting me. And someday, some other young man will be visiting you." That is how it works, this cycle of life, when we know and practice the fifth commandment.

His story reminded me of what God says in Isaiah 46:4 (New International Version):

Even to your old age and gray hairs
I am he, I am he who will sustain you.
I have made you and I will carry you;
I will sustain you and I will rescue you.

How does God sustain us in our old age? How will he carry us and rescue us? I believe it's through our children and others who come alongside us in life. Through the people who honor us, who treat us as important, who listen to us and tell us that our lives still matter and that we are loved.

God's Promise in the Fifth Command

Notice, as the apostle Paul does in the New Testament, that the command to honor your parents is the first of the ten that comes with a promise attached: "Honor your father and your mother *so that your life will be long on the fertile land that Yahweh your God is giving you.*" By honoring our parents and older adults, we model for our children and the generations that follow how they should honor us when we reach "old age" ourselves.

Two months ago, my mother-in-law fell and broke her hip. She's a very sharp, very active eighty-six-year-old, but the injury really set her back. I watched LaVon beautifully care for her mother, sitting with her in the hospital, reassuring her in the rehabilitation center, giving up our bedroom to have her stay with us until she could go home. She fixed meals, talked with nurses, organized her mother's medications, and found ways to encourage her. At a meal recently with our daughters, I said to them, "Girls, I want you to know what a beautiful thing your mom has been doing. I know you've seen part of it, but I want you to know how much she has done to care for your grandmother. I want you to know this because someday, thirty years from now, it might be Mom and I who need your help." They both nodded and told their mother how grateful they felt watching LaVon care for their grandmother. Then, with a laugh, they each promised that the other one would take care of us.

Ray was a retired pastor who visited our congregation shortly after we started meeting in 1990. I knew he was alone—his wife had died years earlier in a tragic car accident. I thought maybe he could use a friend, so I went to visit him and asked if he would help me, as we started the church, by reading scripture on Sundays in worship.

Over the next fifteen years, Ray became a trusted mentor and friend as I navigated the role of pastoring a growing church. At times he challenged me; at times he frustrated me. But I came to value this man and the wisdom he shared that can be gained only by living life. He listened to me when I needed someone to vent to. He shared insights that changed how I thought about life. And the year before he died, he prepared a gift for me.

Ray had an extensive collection of books, classics in theology and scripture, most out of print. He spent hundreds of hours that last year of his life making notes about each book and placing them inside the front covers. Shortly before his death, he invited me over to his house to present this gift to me—more than a thousand books, and a thousand notes telling me what to look for, one inside the front cover of each book. His notes, just a few words, said things like "This is a classic!" or "A great preacher!" or "A great work on suffering and the Christian life."

Later, as Ray lay dying, I sat by his bedside reading scripture, holding his hand, praying for him, and choking back tears as I told him how much I loved him. Fifteen years later, I still open his books as I prepare my sermons. Every time I do, and read the note in his handwriting, I thank God for Ray and the gift he was to me. Honor your father and your mother so that your life will be long on the fertile land that Yahweh your God is giving you.

What Jesus Might Say to You

You are my hands, my feet, my voice. In this commandment my Father is calling you to care not only for your parents and grandparents, your aunts and uncles, but also for older adults who have no one else. He's calling you to visit, to call, to encourage and bless them. You are the means by which I care for the elderly. Honor them, consider them weighty, treat them with respect, and you will find the blessings you've extended will come back to you.

VI

The Tragedy of Violence, the Beauty of Mercy

Do not kill.
—Exodus 20:13

I was leaving Tom and Marcy's house when Tom followed me out to the car.

Two days earlier, the couple's daughter Erin had been shot and killed while attending a popular street festival in downtown Kansas City. She was standing in line at a food truck when, a block away, two teenage boys got into a fight. As one of the boys ran away, he pulled a gun and fired several rounds in the direction of his assailant. None hit his intended target, but one of the stray bullets struck twenty-five-year-old Erin. She died in her boyfriend's arms.

Tom serves as one of our associate pastors, leading our recovery ministry. But long before he'd answered God's call, he and Marcy and their two daughters had been active members of the church. Erin was just six when I became her pastor. This family had served in so many ways to care for others. And now their home was filled with people who'd come to care for them.

As we stood in the driveway, Tom said to me, "Adam, every dad thinks his daughter is special. But Erin really was special. She gave herself to helping and protecting people. How many twenty-five-year-olds chose to work in a battered women's shelter helping others? But she did—she gave herself to help others." With that, he began to weep. I held him in my arms as he repeated over and over again, "Damn it! Damn it! Damn it! Damn it! Damn it!"

Somehow, on that day, Tom's words seemed the most appropriate thing I'd heard in the aftermath of this tragedy.

I've heard well-meaning Christians respond to events like Erin's death by suggesting that the circumstance must have been "the will of God." But from the top of Mount Sinai, Yahweh's voice thundered as he spoke to the Israelites below: DO NOT KILL. *That* is the will of God. Humans are not to take one another's lives. Erin's death, like the thousands of other tragic deaths that happen each day around the world, was not the will of God. Human suffering grieves the heart of God, particularly when it comes in the wake of such violence and such terrible pain.

The prohibition against killing appears in nearly every ancient law code. It has been the most basic of ethical and moral requirements since the beginning of civilization. Yet the last hundred years have been the deadliest in the history of the human race. Over one hundred million people died in combat, and genocidal atrocities saw millions of Jews, Cambodians, Hutus, and countless others slaughtered. More recently, mass shootings have killed children and young adults at schools and concerts and clubs. It seems clear that humanity has utterly failed to abide by this most basic of ethical imperatives.

The commandment, which seems straightforward at first, also raises a host of ethical questions. Does it forbid killing in self-defense? Is it a call to pacifism, or is killing in war ever justified? Is the death penalty permitted? How does it speak to suicide or abortion or euthanasia? I believe the sixth commandment has implications for each of these topics, though it is beyond the scope of this chapter to cover them all. I've addressed the death penalty, euthanasia, and abortion in other books.[1] Here we will consider biblical and ethical arguments related to self-defense, war, and manslaughter before turning to the ways that Jesus broadened the meaning of this command. We'll find that his words have implications far beyond the taking of another human life—words that have power to liberate us from bitterness and resentment and replace them with freedom and joy.

Murder and Killing in the Bible

I wonder how Moses would have heard this commandment, given that he himself had put a man to death for beating Hebrew slaves.

How many times had Moses replayed that act in his memory, during the forty years he lived as a fugitive in the Sinai? Before that event, Moses had been in a unique position to bring about change to Egypt—a prince in Pharaoh's household. What might have happened if, instead of killing the Egyptian taskmaster, he had gone back to Thebes and spent the next forty years working for reform in the treatment of

Egypt's slaves? What *was* Moses feeling when God said from the mountaintop, *Do not kill?*

Moses's story also brings up the question of whether the commandment should read "Do not kill" or "Do not murder." The King James Version has "Thou shalt not kill." Modern translations like the New International Version and the New Revised Standard Version translate the command as "You shall not murder." But the more recent Common English Bible, which I've used primarily throughout this book, returns to "Do not kill."

In Hebrew, the command is made up of only two simple words, *lo tirtzach*. The Hebrew word *tirtzach* is one form of the verb *ratsach*. *Ratsach* appears dozens of times in the Hebrew Bible and is used not only of murder but of manslaughter as well. The Bible recognizes, as our modern law codes do, that there are varying degrees of moral culpability in causing the death of another human being. There is a difference between premeditated murder and accidentally causing the death of another. In both scenarios, there are consequences for killing, but the consequences differ dramatically based upon intent.

Numbers 35 discusses various degrees of moral and criminal culpability for different kinds of homicide. If one strikes another maliciously in a way that is known to lead to death, and the other dies, the act is considered murder and is punishable by death. If, on the other hand, a person strikes another in a way that usually would not lead to death, and death is not intended but nevertheless occurs, provision is made for the individual who committed the crime to flee to a city of asylum. Elsewhere, Exodus 21 dictates what should happen when one person's ox gores and kills a neighbor. If the owner knew the ox was prone to goring, one level of culpability is

guilty
harmful
to blame

assigned. If the owner didn't know the ox was likely to kill, he is still culpable, but at a different level. In every case, the Hebrew Bible demands a penalty when one individual has played a part in the killing of another. But the penalties differ depending upon the circumstances.

It seems clear that the sixth commandment was intended to cover all of these forms of killing, not only first- or even second-degree murder. Yes, the command is telling the Israelites, and us, "Don't murder." But it is also saying, "Don't kill," which prohibits a broader array of actions that might inadvertently lead to the death of someone else, even though this was not the intended outcome.

Murder in the Bible

The Bible's first murder occurs very early in scripture, in Genesis 4. One brother kills another. Both were people of faith, making their offerings to God. Yet despite his faith, Cain killed his brother Abel. Why did Cain kill his brother? He felt jealousy and resentment toward him because "Yahweh looked favorably on Abel and his sacrifice but didn't look favorably on Cain and his sacrifice" (Genesis 4:4–5).

I think you have to read between the lines in this story. How did Cain know that Yahweh looked more favorably on Abel's sacrifice? Is this a euphemism for Abel's relative prosperity compared with Cain's? Did Cain see that Abel was more "blessed" by God, a sign to Cain that Abel's sacrifices were more acceptable to God than his own? In any case, Cain's jealousy, resentment, and bitterness led him to kill his brother. It was murder in the first degree. Yet God showed mercy to Cain. From that time on, life would be hard for

Cain. He would be forced to leave his homeland. Tilling the soil would be more difficult than before. He would live in fear and feel himself hidden from God's presence (see Genesis 4:12–14). Yet God allowed Cain to live and even protected him from harm by others.

Just after the story of Cain and Abel—in the same chapter, as a matter of fact—the Bible records a second act of killing. Lamech, the father of Noah, boasts, "I killed a man for wounding me, a boy for striking me" (Genesis 4:23). Since God promised to protect Cain, Lamech is certain God will give him the same treatment, paying back any who seek to harm him seventy-seven-fold. (Remember this seventy-seven-fold retribution that Lamech hopes God will visit upon those who seek to harm him. We'll come back to it later.)

Fast-forward a chapter, and by Genesis 6, we find the entire world consumed with violence. Killing for resentment, killing for vengeance, killing for fear or hate or desire—it was all part of the ancient world. In Genesis 6:11 we read, "In God's sight, the earth had become corrupt and was filled with violence." Therefore, God said to Noah, "The end has come for all creatures, since they have filled the earth with violence" (Genesis 6:13). Genesis 6:6 describes in such moving terms how God felt when he looked upon the violence on the planet: "Yahweh regretted making human beings on the earth, and he was heartbroken." What follows is the story of the flood.

Other ancient cultures had flood stories. But among the unique features of the biblical account is its emphasis on God's grief about human violence. The flood was a kind of baptism, a cleansing of the earth from its violence with the hope of starting anew with a new family of humans through

Noah. When the waters recede, we read this pronouncement from God:

> Whoever sheds human blood,
> by a human his blood will be shed;
> for in the divine image
> God made human beings. (Genesis 9:6)

Notice that these verses ground the prohibition against killing another human being in the fact that human beings were made in the image of God. This provides a theological basis for human rights in Western civilization. Harming a human being is an offense against God. To kill is to destroy God's possession ("We are his people, the sheep of his own pasture," the Psalmist notes in Psalm 100) and to violate someone who was created in God's image. *Because humans are created in the image of God, created by God and for God, God alone has the authority and right to take a human life.*

Self-Defense and War?

What of self-defense? War? Are we permitted to kill in these situations?

In the field of ethics, there are moral obligations and responsibilities that humans are meant to follow. At times, there will be a conflict between competing duties. As we have just learned, one primary moral obligation is not to kill. But what if we see someone preparing to harm or kill another? Do we have a moral obligation to stop a killing if we can? Even if doing so requires the use of force? A verse that seems to speak to this, at least as it is translated in the CEB, is Leviticus 19:16b: "Do not stand by while your neighbor's blood is shed; I am Yahweh." The verse implies an obligation to intervene to rescue one who is being attacked.

Exodus 22:2 makes clear that protecting one's family and property from a thief is a moral duty that could conflict with the command not to kill: "If the thief is caught breaking in and is beaten and dies, the one who killed him won't be guilty of bloodshed." This verse doesn't encourage bloodshed in the course of self-protection, but it recognizes that if an attack occurs at night, when one can't see the attacker or scare them away, the homeowner is not liable. But the very next verse states, "If this [the thief's entry into the home to steal] happens in broad daylight, then the one who killed him is guilty of bloodshed." In other words, if you are able to stop the thief by an action short of killing them, you must.

Christian just-war theory is based on the premise that there will be times when the command to love your neighbor as you love yourself (Leviticus 19:18) requires one nation or tribe to go to war to protect its own people, or other people, from a hostile attack. Under this theory, war is permitted if it is waged for just reasons and is justly waged.

Even here, war is a sign of human brokenness. It is clear in scripture that God yearns for a world without war. Both Isaiah and Micah draw from a common tradition, positing a longed-for day where there will be no more armed conflict:

> Then they will beat their swords into iron plows
> and their spears into pruning tools.
> Nation will not take up sword against nation;
> they will no longer learn how to make war. (Isaiah 2:4
>   and Micah 4:3)

Isaiah 11 offers another powerful picture of a peaceable kingdom where even the animals will not harm one another:

> The wolf will live with the lamb,
> and the leopard will lie down with the young goat;
> the calf and the young lion will feed together,
> and a little child will lead them.
> The cow and the bear will graze.
> Their young will lie down together,
> and a lion will eat straw like an ox. . . .
> They won't harm or destroy anywhere on my holy
>   mountain.
> The earth will surely be filled with the knowledge of
>   Yahweh,
> just as the water covers the sea. (Isaiah 11:6–7,9)

This picture of a world without violence is a picture of God's ideal world—perhaps even a picture of heaven. It points to a world where no one, not even the animals, kills. But we don't live in that world yet. There will be times when nations will wage war against other nations or their own people. And the Bible, as I and many others read it, allows for nations to take up arms to defend against aggression.

Homicides and Guns

As I was writing this chapter, a forty-three-year-old man walked into a church in Texas, pulled out a rifle, and killed two parishioners before being shot and killed by the head of the church's volunteer security team. The shooter had been battling mental illness. He'd been to the church several times

to receive food. When he walked in on the day of the shoot-
ing, his appearance—dressed in a trench coat and wearing a
fake beard as a disguise—immediately drew the attention of
the security team. Their acts that morning likely saved the
lives of many people.

We can't talk about killing and violence without considering the mass shootings that seem so ubiquitous today. School
shootings, nightclub shootings, shootings at post offices, college campuses, military bases, shopping malls, department
stores, offices, and, yes, churches and synagogues. Each time
it happens, the debate surfaces, like clockwork, over guns.

You know the drill. Immediately some members of Congress, leaders in the community, and others call for stricter
gun laws. Some offer their thoughts and prayers, while on
social media, others snap back that they don't want to hear
about "thoughts and prayers" anymore. Gun rights advocates
remind us that "guns don't kill people; people kill people"
and that "the only way to stop a bad guy with a gun is for a
good guy to have a gun." We're told that "we don't need any
more gun laws; we just need to enforce the laws we've got."
The debate continues. But within days, maybe a week, the
conversation stops and nothing changes.

Let's talk about facts related to homicides in the United
States. In 2018 there were just more than sixteen thousand
homicides in our country. This number is down dramatically
from the early 1980s, when the murder rate was double what
it is today.[2] Our murder rate has fallen back to where it was in
1960, about 5.1 murders per 100,000 people. You are more
than twice as likely to die in a car accident this year as to become a victim of homicide.

Let's consider what we know about who is dying as a result of homicides in the United States. According to FBI sta-

tistics for 2016, 88 percent of those committing murders were men, and 78 percent of those who were killed were men; 83.5 percent of whites who were murdered were killed by whites, and 90.1 percent of blacks killed were killed by blacks.[3] Most of those who committed these crimes were ages seventeen to twenty-nine. Most of the victims were in their twenties and thirties. Finally, a disproportionate number of homicides are committed by low-income people and against low-income people.[4] The demographic most likely to be murdered is young, poor, black men.

Several years ago, we surveyed five thousand people in the congregation I serve about guns and the laws around their use. We found that 34 percent of our people owned guns, while another 14 percent indicated that someone else in the house owned a gun. Forty-one percent who owned a gun had it for personal safety, another 33 percent for hunting, and the rest for various reasons, from collecting to sport to "I'm not sure."

When we asked our congregants if they thought a person should have to take a basic training and gun safety course before purchasing a gun, 86 percent of our gun owners and 96 percent of our non–gun owners said yes. We then looked at private-sale purchases of guns. Currently many can purchase a gun through a private sale, provided it is in their own state, without undergoing a background check. There are websites, a bit like eBay, where you can buy guns from individuals in private sales that, again, do not require background checks. Last time I looked, I found I could purchase either a semiautomatic rifle or a semiautomatic handgun without a license or background check for about $250.

Laws like these have consequences. In 2015 David Ray Conley, who had been barred from legally acquiring a gun because he was a domestic abuser, bought a nine-millimeter handgun through the Internet in a private sale and used it to murder his former girlfriend, her boyfriend, and her six children.[5] When people speak of a private-sale or gun-show loophole, or of closing the loophole on background checks, this is what they are talking about—requiring even those who are selling guns privately to perform background checks, or have someone perform such checks for them. Currently eighteen states require this, but thirty-two do not. In my congregation, 66 percent of gun owners supported the idea of requiring background checks in private sales, as did 92 percent of non–gun owners.

Frazier Glenn Miller, a white supremacist and a felon, would have failed the instant background check currently required at gun shops. But in April of 2014, he went with his friend to Walmart, and his friend purchased a gun for him. This is called a "straw purchase." He then drove to a Jewish community center in Kansas City, planning to kill Jews. Fourteen-year-old Reat Underwood and his grandfather, Dr. William Corporon—both members of the church I serve—were heading into the Jewish community center for tryouts for a talent show. Miller, believing they were Jews, shot and killed them in the parking lot.

The man who purchased the gun for Miller was later found guilty of violating the law. The penalty? A hundred-dollar fine and two years' probation. I asked the five thousand people we surveyed if they would support harsher mandatory penalties to serve as a deterrent for straw sales. Eighty-seven percent of gun owners said they would, as did 94 percent of non–gun owners.

Here's my point in sharing these stories and statistics with you: A vast majority of people, both gun owners and non–

gun owners support basic improvements to gun laws. We're closer in our beliefs than the news would have you believe. There are reasonable gun laws that can make a difference.

As important as better gun laws may be in addressing violent crime, the deeper answer lies elsewhere. Following Erin's death, I spoke with Kansas City's new mayor, Quinton Lucas, about the kind of gun violence that claimed Erin's life. Lucas, a former law professor, was raised in poverty in a single-parent home, fitting the demographic in which so much violence occurs—young, poor, and African American. He said, "The reason I never picked up a gun was that my mother and others told me I was loved. They helped me believe that I had a future and that my life had meaning. If a child feels loved and feels they've got a future, they won't pick up a gun. But if you don't feel you have hope, and you've got nothing to live for, you'll pick up a gun and use it."

Each year, our church invests hundreds of thousands of dollars and thousands of volunteer hours working in partnership with ten elementary schools in the lowest-income communities in the Kansas City metro area. We provide tutoring and books. We rehab school buildings. We provide school supplies and food packs to tide kids over on the weekends. Working closely with the school districts, we aim to give each of these children a belief that they are loved, their lives have meaning, and they have a future.

In watching how these efforts have played out, I've seen that Mayor Lucas was right. One key to curbing violence—and creating a society that reflects God's heart in the sixth command—has to do with helping young people, from the time they're small, know that they are loved, that their lives have meaning, and that they have a future with hope.

Through the Eyes of Jesus

Let's close this chapter by considering what Jesus said about this commandment.

In the Sermon on the Mount, Jesus teaches on the prohibition against killing. Once more he goes behind the letter of the law to the heart of the matter:

> You have heard that it was said to those who lived long ago, *Don't commit murder,* and all who commit murder will be in danger of judgment. But I say to you that everyone who is angry with their brother or sister will be in danger of judgment. If they say to their brother or sister, "You idiot," they will be in danger of being condemned by the governing council. And if they say, "You fool," they will be in danger of fiery hell. (Matthew 5:21–22)

In these words, Jesus makes a connection between anger and the sixth commandment. Most homicides are fueled by anger. The crime is usually not one carefully weighed by the mind but instead the result of passion or a perceived slight. You may never be in danger of committing murder or killing someone, but all of us have been angry with another person. Maybe you've gotten so angry that you feel like telling them off, giving them "the bird," honking your horn at them in the car, or calling them names.

When we were children, our parents taught us what to say when someone else taunted us or called us names. We were to say, "Sticks and stones may break my bones, but words will never hurt me." Was this true? Of course it wasn't. Words can be very painful.

In the passage above, Jesus says we should not say to our brother or sister, "You idiot!" The Greek word for "idiot" is *raka*, which means "empty-headed," "stupid," or "dimwit." He also says not to say to others, "You fool!" The Greek word for fool in Matthew is *more*, from which we have the term "moron."

Perhaps you have other words you use when you are angry with someone, names you call others when you are frustrated. But the point is that when we use words like these, it diminishes someone who was created in the image of God. It dehumanizes them and it dehumanizes you. This is why Jesus extended the sixth commandment to prohibit not just killing others but harming them by way of insult or emotional attack.

Brian's mother worships with our congregation. Brian was a remarkable kid—talented, handsome, full of life. He was also gay. Because of this, he experienced relentless teasing at school. In the hallways, kids would put Post-it notes on his back without his knowing it, notes with cruel words scribbled on them. When he got a car, an exciting day in any teenager's life, someone keyed it. Some of his classmates were relentless, cruel. And one day Brian gave up. He stopped fighting what felt like a lifelong battle to be accepted and loved. And he ended his life. Each person who uttered hurtful words to him had, without intending or realizing it, played a role in his death.

Saint Paul gives a powerful command regarding our words to one another in Ephesians 4:29, a verse I've asked our congregation to memorize. I'd like to encourage you to read it aloud: "Let no evil talk come out of your mouths, but only what is useful for building up, as there is need, so that your words may give grace to those who hear" (Ephesians 4:29,

NRSV). Evil, here, is translated from a Greek word that means "putrid," like rotting food. Imagine finding a Tupperware under the seat of your car with the remains of a casserole you packed a month ago, now completely rotten—that's the word Paul uses to describe the hurtful things we are not to speak to others. Instead, we are to build one another up and ensure that our words give grace—*undeserved kindness*—to all who hear.

We've all had people who hurt us by their words and actions, people whom we might feel justified in lashing out at. Jesus had these same experiences. Religious leaders said that he was possessed by demons and that the powerful things he did to cast out demons were done by the power of the devil. He was rejected by others and ultimately betrayed by a friend. He was beaten and crucified. During his entire ministry, he knew these events were coming. Yet here's what Jesus taught, in a verse I would also encourage you to say out loud:

> You have heard that it was said, *You must love your neighbor* and hate your enemy. But I say to you, love your enemies and pray for those who harass you so that you will be acting as children of your Father who is in heaven. (Matthew 43–45)

This gets to the center of Jesus's ethic: When we read the commandments through the eyes of Jesus, we recognize that the command prohibiting murder is ultimately a command calling for love. Loving one's enemy does not mean summoning warm feelings for them. It is to see them as a human being created in the image of God, and to treat them as you wish they had treated you.

Often this kind of love looks like mercy. Jesus said, "If

anyone strikes you on the right cheek, turn the other also" (Matthew 5:39). When we return blow for blow, we foster a world of violence. But when we return mercy and good for evil, we rob evil and hate of their power. Again, the apostle Paul captured this well when he said, "Don't be defeated by evil, but defeat evil with good" (Romans 12:21).

Our hearts long for vengeance. Jesus teaches forgiveness and empowers us to break the cycle of violence that afflicts our world.

At the beginning of this chapter, I told you the story of Lamech, Noah's father, who promised that whoever bruised or hurt him would receive retribution seventy-seven times. Generations later, Jesus used this very story to make a point about forgiveness.

Once, when Jesus's disciples asked him how to pray, he told them, "Pray, forgive us our trespasses as we forgive those who trespass against us" (Matthew 6:12). When Peter asked Jesus, "Lord, how many times should I forgive my brother or sister who sins against me? Should I forgive as many as seven times?" Jesus replied, "Not just seven times, but rather as many as *seventy-seven times*" (Matthew 18:21–22).

Did you catch that? Lamech vows revenge seventy-seven times, but Jesus teaches us to *forgive* seventy-seven times. Seventy-seven is a way of saying, "You just keep forgiving."

We might think Jesus didn't really know how hard our situation is. If he knew what was done to us, he would not have called us to forgive seventy-seven times. But I want you to recall what Jesus prayed as he hung on the cross being taunted by those who nailed him there: "Father, forgive them, for they don't know what they're doing" (Luke 23:34). We are faced with the same choice as we navigate our lives today.

In 2004 a group of six teens stole a credit card and went shopping. They bought foolish things they didn't need or want—for example, a twenty-pound frozen turkey from a grocery store. As they were driving down the road, just for kicks, nineteen-year-old Ryan Cushing tossed the turkey out his window and into the front windshield of an oncoming car. Behind the wheel of that car was forty-four-year-old Victoria Ruvolo. The frozen projectile burst through her windshield, shattering every bone in her face, crushing her esophagus, and causing brain trauma. Ryan was arrested, and Victoria was taken to the hospital, where she underwent ten hours of surgery. Doctors installed four titanium plates and wire mesh to hold her eye in place. It took nine months of therapy before she could return to work.

After the incident, the district attorney approached Victoria to testify at Ryan's hearing. The young man was looking at a maximum sentence of twenty-five years. Victoria described the day she showed up in court for the sentencing:

> On the day we went to court, I saw this young man walk in wearing a suit which looked like it was three times too big for him; it made him seem so frail. He walked in with his head hung down and looked so upset with himself. When I saw him there, my heart went out to him. To me he looked like a lost soul.

Instead of demanding punishment for this young man, who had caused her immeasurable pain, she asked the judge for amnesty or a reduced sentence. Because of her testimony, the judge gave Cushing six months in prison and five years' probation. Here's how she described what happened after the hearing:

Once the case was over and it was time for him to walk out, he started veering over towards where I was sitting and every court officer was ready to jump on him. They had no idea why he was coming towards me but as he walked over to where I was sitting and stood in front of me, I saw that all he was doing was crying, crying profusely. He looked at me and said, "I never meant this to happen to you, I prayed for you every day. I'm so glad you're doing well." Then this motherly instinct just came over me and all I could do was take him and cuddle him like a child and tell him "just do something good with your life, take this experience and do something good with your life."[6]

Victoria devoted the rest of her life to helping troubled kids and teaching others about the power of forgiveness and letting things go.

Victoria lived the Gospel Jesus preached. She had every right to ask for a harsh punishment. Instead she showed mercy and extended love to the young man who hurt her. This changed not only Ryan but all who heard her story. And in the process, she found freedom from bitterness and resentment and in their place a life of meaning and purpose and a heart filled with love.

Moses taught us, *Do not kill.* But Jesus said it goes deeper than that. Don't harm others. Don't return insult for insult. Forgive others and love your enemies. In doing so, you will find the good and beautiful life.

What Jesus Might Say to You

I know you would never intend to kill. But I'm asking more of you than that. I'm asking you not to harm others with your words or deeds. More than that, I want you to remember that mercy is more powerful than vengeance, just as love is mightier than hate. When you bless those who hurt you, you'll find freedom for your soul, and you might just liberate the other as well.

VII

Faithfulness in an Age of Porn

Do not commit adultery.
—Exodus 20:14

Having worked as a pastor for thirty years, I've heard more than one parishioner confess that they've cheated on their mate. I've also listened to the sorrow, disappointment, and anger of those whose spouses cheated on them. Adultery is a kind of betrayal that violates our deepest trust and usually results in devastating pain.

In the Ten Commandments, the prohibition against adultery follows just after the prohibition against murder, which points to the severity of this transgression against one's neighbor. It is also likely true that the inclusion of this command indicates that infidelity was a common occurrence among the ancient Israelites, just as it was among the ancient Egyptians and every other ancient people.[1] Prohibitions against adultery are found in nearly every ancient legal code.

The fear that one's spouse had cheated must have been

prevalent enough that Numbers 5:11–31 outlines a process used by the priests to determine if a woman had cheated on her husband. The code says she should undergo a test that would force her to miscarry if found to be carrying another man's child. Later in scripture, Proverbs 6 and 7 provide stern warnings to men against sleeping with another man's wife.

Adultery was a metaphor regularly used by the prophets to describe Israel's infidelity to God. In these passages, Israel was portrayed as an unfaithful wife, and God as Israel's faithful husband. As Israel violated the first two commandments, worshipping other gods and making use of idols, she was said to have committed adultery against God. Hence God said to the Jewish people:

> How can I pardon you?
> Your children have forsaken me
> and swear by gods that are not gods.
> Although I could have satisfied them,
> they committed adultery,
> dashing off to the prostitution house. (Jeremiah 5:7)

Adultery was such a serious violation of God's will that, in the Law of Moses, it was punishable by death. Leviticus 20:10 states, "If a man commits adultery with a married woman, committing adultery with a neighbor's wife, both the adulterer and the adulteress must be executed." Deuteronomy 22:22 repeats the command in slightly more direct terms: "If a man is found having sex with a woman who is married to someone else, both of them must die—the man who was having sex with the woman and the woman herself."

In the passages above, you may have noticed that adultery was framed as a sin committed against a married *man* by his wife and another man. By contrast, a husband did not commit adultery against his wife when he slept with another woman. In patriarchal and polygynous societies, a married man might have more than one wife and dozens of concubines (secondary-status wives). He might even sleep with an unmarried woman without its being considered adultery.[2] Adultery was, technically, a violation of a husband's rights that took place when another man slept with his wife. Far from being unique to Israel, this definition was nearly universal in the ancient Near East.

Note, though, how the idea of patriarchy—men holding primary legal rights and power in society—was absent in the Bible's opening story of creation in Genesis 1. There we read:

> God created humanity in God's own image,
> in the divine image God created them,
> male and female God created them. (Genesis 1:27)

In Genesis 1, men and women were created *at the same time* and each in the image of God. Further, God says to the man *and* the woman, "Be fertile and multiply; fill the earth and master it. Take charge of the fish of the sea, the birds in the sky, and everything crawling on the ground" (Genesis 1:28). According to this text, men and women were to rule together in partnership, with no sign of patriarchy.

Patriarchy arises in the Bible's second creation account, in Genesis 2:4b–3:24. This creation story is written in a markedly different way from the first one. Genesis 1 was written in the form of Hebrew poetry, and the creation story found there is something like a creed or liturgy—it points to the goodness of God and all that God had made. Genesis 2:4b and the following verses were written in prose, telling a narrative story. In this more "earthy" portrait, human beings were created not by God's speaking them into existence but by God forming them from the dust of the earth.

In the second creation story, the woman is created after the man as God's response to Adam's loneliness. God says, "It's not good that the human is alone. I will make him a helper that is perfect for him" (Genesis 2:18). In this account, God takes a rib from the man's side and forms the woman. God blesses the first humans with the Garden of Eden but warns them not to eat the fruit from the tree of the knowledge of good and evil. A few verses later, the woman is persuaded by a talking serpent to eat the forbidden fruit. She eats and in turn gives the fruit to her husband to eat.

When God discovers their disobedience, he expels the humans from paradise. He tells Adam that henceforth the earth will be more difficult to cultivate and harvest relative to the ease with which food was available in Eden. And he tells Eve that childbirth will now be more painful and that "You will desire your husband, but he will rule over you" (Genesis 3:16).

In both creation accounts, it appears that in Eden the man did not rule over the woman, but they shared the partnership described in Genesis 1. I believe that patriarchy and the subordination of women in human society were never God's will. Genesis 3:16 was not prescriptive. Rather, the verse was descriptive—it was announcing how things would be in a broken world outside of Eden. It is how relationships would be distorted by sin and the difference in physical strength generally seen between the genders. This patriarchy was seen as normative across the ancient world. But it was not God's original or intended will. And when Christians pray, "Thy kingdom come, thy will be done, on earth as it is in heaven," we are praying for, among other things, the end of patriarchy and a return to the partnership seen in Genesis 1.

Before turning to Jesus's words concerning the seventh commandment, let's consider the best-known example of adultery in the Hebrew Bible, the infamous story of King David's adultery with Bathsheba, the wife of Uriah.

The Anatomy of an Affair

David was viewed in scripture as Israel's greatest king. The Bible mentions him more often than anyone except Jesus, and God himself identified David as "a man after his own heart" (1 Samuel 13:14 and Acts 13:22, NRSV). He was a courageous warrior who ruled with a shepherd's care for his people and a deep faith that he expressed through poetry that we still read in the Psalms today. Yet despite this, David also experienced temptation and, in this case, ultimately succumbed to it.

The story begins in springtime. David sent his army off to war to fight against the Ammonites. "*But David remained in Jerusalem,*" the text says (2 Samuel 11:1b, emphasis added). David had always led his men into battle. Yet this time he sent his men to fight while he remained in his citadel. The mention of David remaining behind is, I believe, meant to point to a change in the shepherd-king's heart. Perhaps it was pride or a sense of entitlement that led him to stay behind in his palace while others fought on his behalf.

"One evening," the story continues, "David got up from his couch and was pacing back and forth on the roof of the palace. From the roof he saw a woman bathing; the woman was very beautiful" (2 Samuel 11:2). If you visit Jerusalem, you can see what archaeologists believe are the foundation walls of David's palace. His home would have been the highest building in Jerusalem at the time. From his room he could easily look down upon the homes of his neighbors.

That night, David saw the beautiful Bathsheba bathing. Rather than turn away, as decency would dictate, he kept looking. It seems that in the days that followed, he could not stop thinking about this woman. Here I'm reminded of the words of the Epistle of James:

> Everyone is tempted by their own cravings; they are lured away and enticed by them. Once those cravings conceive, they give birth to sin; and when sin grows up, it gives birth to death. (James 1:14–15)

David knew the commandments we have been studying in this book. But he entertained his desires. They were allowed to gestate until they finally gave birth to actions.

Author and pastor Walter Wangerin once wrote about "the moment of 'maybe,'"[3] the split second in which we may be seized by the thought of having an intimate relationship with someone who is not our spouse. When the thought crosses our mind, we either immediately shut the door—recognizing that an affair is wrong, is prohibited by God, and will result in pain—or we entertain the idea. We cultivate it. We imagine what it might be like. At this point, we might not have any intention of actually cheating on our mate or violating someone else's marriage vows. Perhaps that's how David felt as he watched Bathsheba on the roof that night. The problem, Wangerin notes, is that when we begin to play with "maybe," it can be a short walk to "yes."

"David sent someone and inquired about the woman.

The report came back: 'Isn't this Eliam's daughter Bathsheba, the wife of Uriah the Hittite?'" (2 Samuel 11:3). At this point, David still had not violated the commandment. He simply wanted to know more about the woman he'd seen bathing. But when he found out that she was Eliam's daughter and the wife of Uriah, one of his warriors fighting the Ammonites, that should have been the end of his interest. Instead we read, "So David sent messengers to take her. When she came to him, he had sex with her" (2 Samuel 11:4).

Carefully notice the words here. David's messengers "take" Bathsheba, then David has sex with her. Generations of men have read this story imagining that Bathsheba willingly came to see the king, flattered and excited to be invited to the palace. They assumed Bathsheba willingly slept with David, drawn to him as he was to her. But that is not what the text says. Instead it seems likely to many interpreters that David's taking and having sex with this young woman whose husband was off at war was not born of mutual desire.

In the story, Bathsheba appears to have no children yet. She is likely in her teens, while David is likely in his fifties. He is the king. She is the wife of a foreigner, giving her a somewhat lower status than the wife of an Israelite in this ancient culture. Can she say no? If so, at what cost? When you dig beneath the surface, the account from the Bible sounds tragically familiar to the stories we've frequently heard in this #MeToo era: a powerful man forcing himself upon a woman under a stated or implied threat.

The next time we hear from Bathsheba, a month has passed. She sends word to David that she has missed her period. She's pregnant. David, now realizing his sin could be made public, and knowing the severity of the seventh commandment, seeks to hide his sin.

The king sends for Bathsheba's husband, Uriah, under the pretense of wanting a report from the front lines of the war. Uriah returns, giving his report, after which David urges Uriah to go home and enjoy an evening with his wife. David hopes Uriah will sleep with his wife and believe, when the child is born eight months later, that the baby is his own. But Uriah is too honorable to sleep with his wife while his fellow soldiers are on the war front. Instead he sleeps on the front step of the palace to guard the king. When David hears this the next day, he tries to get Uriah drunk so that he will go home and sleep with Bathsheba. But this backup plan also fails. Uriah holds on to his honor and the commitment he made to his men.

And this is where one sin begets another. David, afraid of his sin being found out, hatches a plan. He prepares a letter to Joab, his general on the front lines: "Place Uriah at the front of the fiercest battle, and then pull back from him so that he will be struck down and die." He seals the letter and asks Uriah to take it back to the general. Uriah has no idea that the letter he carries is his own death sentence. Joab does as the king commands, and Uriah dies in battle. When the news makes it back to Jerusalem, David plays the part of the compassionate king, marrying Uriah's poor widow—what would seem to others an act of remarkable kindness on the part of the shepherd king.

It would be easier to read this story if David were simply an evil person. But he's one of the Bible's heroes. His story is told across four books of the Hebrew Bible. Seventy-three of the Psalms are attributed or dedicated to David. Jesus is called "the son of David"—a messianic title—twelve times in the Gospels. The story is a reminder that if someone as seemingly pious as David can succumb to adultery, so can the rest of us. Here I appreciate the words of Aleksandr Solzhenitsyn: "If only there were evil people somewhere insidiously committing evil deeds, and it were necessary only to separate them from the rest of us and destroy them. But the line dividing good and evil cuts through the heart of every human being."[4] Whether it's murder, adultery, or a violation of any of the other commandments we'll examine in the next few chapters, all of us are capable of evil.

Jesus Redefines Adultery

Not only did Jesus greatly expand the meaning of this command, but he also upended the practice of patriarchy behind its traditional legal definition.

In the Sermon on the Mount, Jesus says, "You have heard that it was said, *Don't commit adultery.* But I say to you that every man who looks at a woman lustfully has already committed adultery in his heart" (Matthew 5:27–28). Note that Jesus doesn't specify whether the woman is married or not. Remarkably, Jesus says that adultery includes not only the act of intercourse with a woman who is not one's wife but also the desire behind the act. He recognizes the importance of the "moment of maybe."

Jesus goes on to say:

And if your right eye causes you to fall into sin, tear it out and throw it away. It's better that you lose a part of your body than that your whole body be thrown into hell. And if your right hand causes you to fall into sin, chop it off and throw it away. It's better that you lose a part of your body than that your whole body go into hell. (Matthew 5:29–30)

Does he really intend us to pluck out our eyes or cut off our hands? No. Jesus often speaks in what is called "prophetic hyperbole." "Prophetic" refers to bold statements addressing what is or is not God's will. "Hyperbole" means intentionally exaggerating to make a point ("I'm so hungry I could eat a horse" is a common example). In Matthew 5, Jesus is clear that we're not meant to objectify others or to entertain illicit desires in our hearts. He also recognizes that sin begins with the "maybe" that we ponder in our hearts. And his mention of cutting off hands and plucking out eyes? It was a way of saying, "This is serious. Pursue this path of desire and it could destroy you and others."

I'm reminded of Jimmy Carter's famous words when he spoke to *Playboy* magazine during his 1976 campaign for the White House:

Christ set some almost impossible standards for us. Christ said, "I tell you that anyone who looks on a woman with lust has in his heart already committed adultery." I've looked on a lot of women with lust. I've committed adultery in my heart many times. This is something that God recognizes I will do—and I have done it—and God forgives me for it.[5]

As Carter said, there are very few men, and perhaps few women as well, who have not violated this command as Jesus defines it.

Surviving the Moment of the "Maybe"

As a young man, I thought about sex all the time. This was in part a function of biology, raging hormones that I had no control over. These desires didn't suddenly cease when I became a Christian at the age of fourteen. Getting married didn't instantly make me uninterested in all other women I met. There have been times across the course of my married life when thoughts of "maybe" raced through my brain and sought to burrow their way into my heart.

I've seen more than a dozen colleagues in ministry give in to the "moment of maybe." I feel compassion for their mates and the pain they've experienced. Some of their marriages survived; many did not. I also recognize how easy it would have been at points in my life to have followed in their footsteps.

LaVon and I have been married for thirty-eight years. Our wedding took place the week after I graduated from high school—not usually the wisest age to get married. We've fallen out of love with each other several times across those thirty-eight years. She's noted that there have been times when the church seemed like my mistress, seasons when I allowed the demands of the ministry to become all-consuming. I would have meetings every night of the week, and even when I was home I could easily be preoccupied in my focus on sermons or ministries or people I needed to care for. I tried to be engaged at home. I scheduled date nights with LaVon and my girls and sought to prioritize them. But it didn't always work out that way, or feel that way to them. And then there were the books, like the one you are holding in your hand. Those were written on my days off, late at night, and on vacations.

In those seasons, I would come home from work excited and energized. I would share with LaVon the new ministries we were planning, or the important things that had happened in my day, or the insights I'd discovered working on my sermon. She'd often listen with enthusiasm, but when she was feeling unvalued, she would say, "Really? Do we have to talk about the church all the time?"

I'd feel shot down and discouraged. But when I went back to the office, I was no longer Adam Hamilton, failing husband, but Adam Hamilton, caring pastor and visionary leader seeking to accomplish great things for God. In those seasons, our personal and intimate life suffered and the word "maybe" once more entered my vocabulary. Likewise, if someone had come along in those moments when LaVon felt alone and uncared for—someone who paid attention to her and who made her feel loved and valued—it would have been easy for her to have been drawn into a relationship with someone else. Thankfully, that didn't happen for either of us.

In caring for friends and congregants who have been through affairs, I have seen that when a person is drifting into adultery, they are often blind to the consequences that will result. Even clergy whose careers, ministries, and congregations will be wrecked by an affair cannot see this in the moment. Perhaps for LaVon and me, it was having witnessed those consequences that kept us faithful to each other. That and the grace of God. More than once we recognized we were struggling. I would pull back on work, and she would turn toward me instead of away. We'd pray for each other and remember the calling to be each other's helpers and companions. And over time, we'd find that "loving feeling" again.

Feelings of love come and go. The commitment we make in marriage is not to always *feel* in love. It is to always *practice* love; to seek to bless, encourage, and build up our mate. Those seasons of resentment or frustration or loveless days and nights are like the "check engine" light in a car. They are not signs that the car needs to be sent to the scrap yard, only that it needs some help. Often the underlying problem is relatively minor, but sometimes it's big enough that you can't fix it on your own. At one point, LaVon and I sought professional counseling—someone who could help us understand the underlying causes of the particular "check engine" light we were experiencing.

Today, thirty-eight years in, we are more in love with each other than we have ever been, and enjoying the best seasons of our life—empty nest, a beautiful granddaughter, a bit of travel. We looked at each other the other day and agreed, "We're so glad we never gave up."

The Prevalence of Infidelity

How common is infidelity today? The 2018 General Social Survey out of the University of Chicago asked the question (as it has each year since 1972) "Is it wrong to have sex with someone other than your spouse?" Seventy-six percent of married persons said it is always wrong, and another 15 percent said it is almost always wrong. That's about the same number of people who indicated that affairs were wrong in 1970 (though the number who say adultery is always wrong is down 10 percent from the 1980s).

So most people agree that infidelity is wrong, but many have had affairs nonetheless. The numbers from national studies vary widely, but looking at the General Social Survey data on those currently married, the numbers range from about 16 percent of those in their sixties and seventies to about 10 percent of those in their twenties, thirties, and forties and about 12 percent of those in their fifties.[6] Other surveys suggest that as many as 20 percent of married persons have had at least one affair, with a handful reporting even higher numbers. It's worth noting that these numbers are far lower than estimates from the past. It appears from the GSS that younger generations are becoming less inclined to have an affair, though the numbers are rising slightly among middle-aged and older adults.

Still, some websites and blogs extol the "benefits" of having an affair. Even after a scandal in which the identities of millions of its users were leaked, Ashley Madison—a dating site for married people—continues to claim sixty million users who have bought into its marketing slogan, "Life is short. Have an affair." As appealing as this might sound, the reality is that your life is not so short. Most of us will grow old, and there is something beautiful about doing so with a partner and friend who has stood at your side for your entire life. But while your life is not short, your marriage likely will be when you pursue an affair. The hurt and pain that result from adultery always outweigh the benefits.

Having said that: It is easy to understand how good people, who genuinely love God and love their mates, end up in another's embrace. I remember speaking to a woman who had just confessed her affair to me. She described the emptiness of her marriage, a husband who was never home, never noticed, never told her she was loved or special or beautiful. Eventually she met another man who did tell her these things, and they ended up sleeping together. She knew it was wrong and had broken it off quickly. But she wept as she told me of the heartache she felt, the guilt and the shame. Her deepest hope was that she could put her marriage back together again.

I think also of a man, in his early forties at the time, who confessed his affair to me. It started as a flirtatious relationship at the office, seemingly innocent. But the excitement and energy of the forbidden relationship led the man and woman, both leaders in their churches, to a hotel room one night. They pledged they would never do it again, but the lure was too great.

When the affair was found out, he said it was like waking from a stupor. He did not love the woman he'd been sleeping with. He loved his wife. But he'd caused her such pain, destroyed her sense of self-worth and her trust. He sobbed in my office, asking if there was any way he could heal the harm he'd caused to the woman with whom he'd always dreamed of growing old.

My point in sharing these two stories, out of the dozens I know, is to remind you both of your vulnerability and of the consequences we often can't see when we're wrestling with the "maybe." I've often thought that I know of no one who, if you were to put them in the wrong situation at the wrong time in their lives, couldn't be seriously tempted to have an affair. And the challenge is even greater when we consider another temptation that's readily available today: pornography.

Pornography and Adultery

Pornography has become ubiquitous in our Internet age, but it is by no means a modern phenomenon. The ruins of ancient Pompeii, a city frozen in time by the eruption of Mount Vesuvius in A.D. 79, make clear that sexually explicit images were a part of the ancient world. And the surprisingly high proportion of brothels to residents of the city makes modern cities appear Victorian by comparison.

But it is the ease and anonymity with which one can view pornography today—not simply images but video—and the staggering amount of this content that is easily accessible that separate ours from prior periods of human history. In 2019 the largest porn site in the world noted that it had 42 *billion* visits that year. (Bear in mind that there are just over seven billion people on our planet.) It averaged 115 million visits to its site per day, an increase of 15 percent over 2018. Over the last twelve months, the company noted, 6.83 *million* new pornographic videos had been uploaded to its site. These numbers are mind numbing.

Recent studies of the impact of pornography use have found that there is an inverse relationship between porn use and sexual satisfaction.[7] The more frequently individuals of both genders viewed porn, the less satisfying they found their sexual relationship with their mate. There are correlations between porn use and divorce among young adults.[8] A recent study of 6,463 Polish college students found that 58.7 percent felt pornography had a negative impact on social relationships and 63.9 percent felt its use had a negative impact on mental health.[9]

The British edition of *Cosmopolitan* ran an article recently about "porn-induced erectile dysfunction"—PIED for short. It noted that a significant number of British young men aged eighteen to twenty-five found it hard to climax during sexual intercourse with a woman due to frequent use of pornography and masturbation. The article quoted neuroscientist Nicola Ray of Manchester Metropolitan University:

> Porn works on the brain like any addictive substance. . . .
> The thing you're addicted to takes hold of your neural
> circuitry and hijacks the pathways related to more natural
> rewards so that they become unresponsive. So porn be-
> comes the only thing the brain understands in relation to
> sexual stimulation; basically real sex becomes increasingly
> less exciting.[10]

Is every user of pornography affected by PIED? No. But for many who frequently use pornography for self-stimulation, the level of stimulation provided by multiple images and videos produced by actors and actresses pretending to engage in sexual activity that real couples do not engage in makes it difficult for real sexual intimacy to measure up.

I've heard parishioners describe how the regular use of porn led them to escalating "levels" of pornographic material in order to achieve climax. In some cases, this led young adults to have unrealistic expectations of what sexual behavior should be like with a mate. In other cases, viewing pornography led individuals to pursue real-life actions that were harmful to themselves or others, and sometimes even illegal. Increasing rates of unwanted "rough" sex reported by women is one example. Another is consumption of child pornography and other forms of child sexual abuse.

The New York Times recently noted, "Last year, tech companies reported 45 million online photos and videos of children being sexually abused—more than double what they found the previous year."[11] Where is the appetite and desire for this kind of illegal and horrific material coming from? Do the people who view these images and videos start off with child porn? Or do they begin with more "normal" pornography and gradually escalate to this?

I remember speaking with a man who had been convicted of possession of child pornography. For him there was a clear through line from his use of "normal" porn to his addiction to pornography and ultimately to his search for more and more deviant images that led to his use of child pornography. This man, now in recovery, had always considered himself a follower of Christ. He felt deeply ashamed of what he was doing and yet found it very hard to stop. His story gave new meaning to Jesus's words "If your eye causes you to sin, pluck it out." While Jesus didn't mean this literally, he was pointing to the idea that the things we train our eyes upon can destroy us.

I've only scratched the surface of reasons not to use pornography. Yet porn seems ubiquitous and so easily accessible that its use is an increasing challenge for large numbers of Christians.

I have no judgment for those who use Internet pornography—large percentages of the population, according to some studies. I spoke with one man in my congregation who struggled with the guilt and shame that accompanied his struggle with "ordinary" porn. He told me, "I feel like I shouldn't even be coming to church. I am such a failure. God knows how often I've failed. I try really hard to refrain, and a few days go by, maybe a week or two, and then I find myself succumbing once more to the desire. How could God possibly love me?"

My response to him was "God knows your desire and your struggle. He's seen every time you failed. He doesn't want this for you. But I wonder if, while you focus on every time you failed, God sees every day that you thought about viewing porn but didn't. He knows you resisted on those days precisely because you love him. That doesn't mean he doesn't care about the times you failed. But remember that he also sees the times you have overcome."

Thoughts on Resisting Temptation

Over the years, dozens of people have shared with me their stories of affairs. Hundreds more have talked about their struggles with other forms of temptation and what they have done to resist. When placed alongside the Bible's teachings, several common tactics emerge that seem to help in resisting temptation. I think of these as the Five Rs of Resisting Temptation:

1. **Remember who you are:** Who are you? What roles do you hope define you? (For me, I am a Christ follower, LaVon's husband, Danielle and Rebecca's dad, Stella's grandpa, and Resurrection's pastor. I want to be defined as someone who loves God, follows Jesus, and loves others, starting with my family.) Is the action I am tempted by consistent with these roles and characteristics that I hope define me?

2. **Recognize the consequences of the action:** What are the worst possible consequences of saying yes to this temptation? How would I feel after saying yes—proud or ashamed? Who would be hurt if my actions were discovered, and how would it impact them?

3. **Rededicate yourself to God:** In the midst of the temptation, pause to pray and recommit yourself to

God. James famously noted, "Resist the devil, and he will run away from you" (James 4:7). Resisting the devil is easiest when we ask for God's help and recommit ourselves to him. When you do this, it acts like a cold shower in the "moment of maybe."

4. **Reveal your struggle to a trusted friend:** As long as something remains a secret, it has power over us. But when we share our secret temptation with someone else, the desire often dissipates. The friend will be able to hold you accountable. Enlist your friend's support. If this is your mate, share your passwords with them and invite them to monitor your Internet search history, your texts and email or your credit card bills. LaVon has always had access to all of my accounts and my phone. If I need to hide something from her, I shouldn't be doing it.

5. **Remove yourself from the tempting situation:** This may be as simple as using Google's SafeSearch feature to block explicit content on your computer or installing porn-blocking software on your phone. It might mean unfriending people or breaking off relationships in the workplace, neighborhood, or even church, if you find yourself developing unhealthy emotional relationships. In some cases, it could mean doing something as serious as leaving a job or moving.

The last of these suggestions may seem extreme, until we consider the cost of succumbing to certain temptations. Having seen infidelity cost people their marriages, their relationships with their children, their homes and careers, I've come to believe it would have been less costly for them to take a new job or move than to have stayed in the situation that destroyed their family.

We began this chapter talking about King David's infidelity. I'd like to end by looking at another famous example of infidelity, a woman caught in the act of adultery. Her story, and Jesus's response to her, is found in the eighth chapter of the Gospel of John.

Let the One Who Is Without Sin Cast the First Stone

In John 8 there is a well-known story that was not originally a part of John's Gospel. Scholars believe it was an authentic story about Jesus that circulated among Christians until it was added to John's Gospel in the second century. According to this account, Jesus was teaching in the temple courts when

> the legal experts and Pharisees brought a woman caught in adultery. Placing her in the center of the group, they said to Jesus, "Teacher, this woman was caught in the act of committing adultery. In the Law, Moses commanded us to stone women like this. What do you say?" (John 8:3–5)

It was, of course, a trap. They had seen Jesus show mercy toward "sinners and tax collectors." How would Jesus respond to a situation in which scripture clearly calls for the death penalty? I believe they anticipated that Jesus would compromise on the "authority of scripture" in favor of showing mercy to this woman.

Can you imagine what the woman must have felt? She was terrified, humiliated, and utterly exposed. We don't know much about her story. Was she in a loveless or abusive marriage and found herself drawn to another man who expressed genuine love for her? Or was she, like Bathsheba, forced into sex by a powerful man who had power over her? We don't know. And where was the man who was committing adultery with her? Why did the Pharisees not bring him to Jesus?

The author of this Gospel fragment tells us, "Jesus bent down and wrote on the ground with his finger." Jesus did this twice, in verses 6 and 8. It is a mystery what Jesus wrote, but Jerome, writing in the fourth or early fifth century, suggested that he was writing in the dirt the sins of the religious leaders.

As the religious leaders continued to question him, Jesus stood up and spoke. "Whoever hasn't sinned should throw the first stone," he said. One by one, the religious leaders dropped their stones and walked away. What a brilliant answer. He doesn't set aside the scripture that calls adultery a serious sin. But he points to the reality that we have all sinned. Contrary to what you might have heard, all sin is not equal. The Bible itself makes this clear. But even here, on one of the "top ten" sins, Jesus shows mercy.

The story continues, "Finally, only Jesus and the woman were left in the middle of the crowd. Jesus stood up and said to her, 'Woman, where are they? Is there no one to condemn you?' She said, 'No one, sir.' Jesus said, 'Neither do I condemn you. Go, and from now on, don't sin anymore.'" (The entire story is found in John 8:2–10.)

Jesus set impossible standards in his teachings and ministry. He forbade us from even looking at another with lust in our hearts. Yet when a woman was caught in the very act of adul-

Faithfulness in an Age of Porn   157

tery, Jesus refused to condemn her. He looked at this woman with compassion. He understood her humanity and whatever circumstances had led her to the embrace of a man who was not her husband.

Jesus forgave her and forced her accusers to set her free. What does that tell us about his mercy toward us?

While this story may not have been part of John's Gospel, I'm so grateful the second-century church inserted it. It is one of the stories that lead me to love Jesus—both for his response to the hypocrisy of the religious leaders and for the love he showed the woman in the most vulnerable moment of her life.

What was true for this woman is also true for me and you. The Lord's forgiveness might not eliminate the consequences of our actions. A marriage can survive infidelity, though it requires remarkable mercy, patience, and love, and usually help from a counselor. But whether our marriage survives or not, Jesus reminds us in this story that God is rich in mercy and "abounding in steadfast love" (Exodus 34:6, NRSV).

What Jesus Might Say to You

I understand. I understand how powerful your desires are. I felt these desires when I walked the earth. And I understand how accessible and available temptations are to you. Remember, I taught you to pray, "Lead us not into temptation." Know that my Father will not lead you into temptation, but as you pray these words, he will help you resist and lead you on another path, better than the one you are tempted by. Know that our "no" is not for lack of love for you. It is not to keep you from pleasure or satisfaction. Our "no" is to keep you from harm, from shame, from pain. We want what is best for you. Resist the dark side, the tempter, and the temptation you are drawn to. The tempter and the temptation are not irresistible. Remember who you are—you are my Father's beloved child and you are my disciple. We don't want you to experience the pain of infidelity, nor to inflict it upon someone else. But know this too: If you have fallen and given in to desire, know that I am willing and able to forgive you.

VIII

We're All Thieves. Yes, Even You.

Do not steal.
—Exodus 20:15

When I was ten, I saved my money to buy Elton John's *Greatest Hits* on vinyl. I rode my bike to the Jones Store, a large department store a couple of blocks from my home, and went straight to the record department to find the album. To my dismay, the price was $5.98. I'd thought it was $4.98, like most other albums in those days. I had only enough to buy the album for $4.98 plus tax. I was $1 short.

Instead of going home, I had a devious thought. Why not replace the price tag with one from another album that was at the lower price? My heart beat like crazy as I looked around the store. No clerks were in sight, so I carefully peeled a price tag from another album and placed it over the tag on the Elton John album. Then I carried it to the register and waited for a clerk to show up. This was forty-six years ago, but I can still feel the tension of that moment. The cashier finally arrived at the register and rang me up for $4.98. I walked out with my album and a lot of remorse.

I learned that day that I would never make a good thief—though, as I'll suggest later in this chapter, the Elton John heist would not be my last theft. But the guilt I was feeling, and the innate sense of shame, did keep me from ever switching price tags again.

The eighth commandment, like several of the other commandments, might seem at first so obvious as to appear nearly irrelevant to us. Surely we don't need to spend time exploring what it means not to steal. All who agree that stealing is wrong, say "aye." Opposed, "nay." The vote passes unanimously. Few people think stealing is okay, and most of us would not consider ourselves thieves.

Yet in the ancient Near East, every law code we know of included a prohibition against theft. When we find a law so universal in adoption among ancient people, it suggests that the problem was widespread and needed to be addressed. Generally, laws were written in response to acts that were considered egregious and needed to be regulated. We can assume that stealing made it onto the "top ten" list on the two tablets both because it was deemed serious and because it was a problem in the early Israelite community.

In this chapter, I want to suggest that the same is true of us today. When we look at the applications of this commandment in the Bible, there are a wide array of activities that fall under the category of theft—choices you and I face on a daily basis. We'll consider these, and then we'll turn to the words of Jesus, who not only calls us to refrain from stealing but empowers us to practice its opposites: generosity and selfless love.

With this in mind, let's consider the eighth commandment in its original context.

Finders, Keepers?

As a kid, you may have learned the saying, "Finders, keepers; losers, weepers." The idea was simple. If you find something that isn't yours, you can keep it. It's not your fault that the owner lost the item. You find a hundred-dollar bill on the ground. What do you do? Many people would try to find the rightful owner. Some would consider it their lucky day and not think twice about keeping the money.

In Israelite society, "finders, keepers" amounted to taking what wasn't yours. This was especially important in an agrarian society where sheep and goats had a tendency to wander off. In Exodus 23:4–5 we read,

> When you happen to come upon your enemy's ox or donkey that has wandered off, you should bring it back to them. When you see a donkey that belongs to someone who hates you and it's lying down under its load and you are inclined not to help set it free, you must help set it free.

These verses outline two different ethical requirements, but they are linked. You are to return what you find that belongs to another. That is what it means to be a neighbor. Keeping what you found would be stealing. Then scripture takes the principle a step further. If even your enemy, or someone who hates you, has an animal in trouble, you are to help it. You do this because this is the very thing you would hope someone would do for your animals if they were lost or in distress. You can hear echoes of this idea in Jesus's Golden Rule, "Do to others as you would have them do to you" (Matthew 7:12, NRSV), as well as his call to "love your enemies" (Matthew 5:44 and Luke 6:27,35).

On a trip to Egypt, traveling through the wilderness on the way to Mount Sinai, I saw a stray camel. When I asked my guide about this camel, he said, "Every camel you find here, every sheep and every goat, belongs to someone. When an animal wanders off, and someone else finds the animal, they always take it back to its rightful owner. This is life among the Bedouin. This is how they live." Today's Bedouin live much as the Israelites did 3,300 years ago. And they practice the same ethic God gave to the Israelites on Sinai: "Do not take what does not belong to you." In other words, "No, finders are not keepers."

The first time I visited Egypt, I stayed at the Meridien Hotel across from the pyramids. It was late when I checked in, and I went to tip the porter who had brought my luggage to the room. I gave him what I thought was five one-dollar bills. He thanked me and went back to the lobby.

After unpacking, I went to the lobby restaurant to grab a bite to eat. I sat down and was soon approached again by the porter, who had tracked down my guide to translate. The porter said something in Arabic, and my guide translated, "I don't think you intended to give me this." The porter then handed me a hundred-dollar bill.

Apparently when I gave the porter what I thought was a five-dollar tip, I gave him four one-dollar bills and a hundred-dollar bill. I'd brought only three hundred dollars in cash for the entire two-week trip. I thanked him profusely and tried giving him an additional tip for returning the money, but he would not accept it.

I was floored. This young Egyptian could have kept the hundred-dollar bill, and I never would have known where I'd lost it. But he did not want to take advantage of me. Character, honesty, and integrity were what I saw in him and in the other Egyptians I met on that trip.

A friend once faced the same decision after going through the drive-through at his local bank. He deposited a check and requested two hundred dollars in cash back. The young teller was obviously new; he didn't count the money before stuffing it into the envelope and handing it to my friend. My friend pulled away, then decided he should count what was in the envelope. That's when he discovered the young man had given him four hundred dollars back, twenty twenties instead of twenty tens. He turned back around and returned it to the teller, who was both embarrassed and very grateful.

What price do you place on your integrity? For the Bedouin, the camel is returned. For my Egyptian porter, the hundred dollars is given back. For my friend at the bank, the two hundred dollars was returned to the teller. Each time you find something that isn't yours, or you are unintentionally given something that you were not meant to have, it is a test of your character.

That's the positive intent of the eighth commandment. It looks a lot like the Golden Rule, "Do unto others as you would have them do unto you." Still, it's a relatively clear interpretation. But how does this command apply to those of us who wouldn't think of taking or keeping something that isn't ours?

Stepping on *Your* Toes

I began this chapter with fifth-grade Adam Hamilton switching the labels on an Elton John record. Maybe you did something like that, and maybe you didn't. But you can excuse me for doing it, because I was just ten years old, and it was just a dollar that I stole. I've grown a lot since then.

Then there's the "finders, keepers" ethic. Maybe you know people who would keep the hundred-dollar bill if someone handed it to them mistakenly, but you know *you* would return it. And of course, there's ordinary thieving—taking someone's donkey or bicycle or cellphone. None of us would do that.

So now allow me to step on *your* toes (and mine) by seeing if I can find your violation of the eighth commandment. And when I find it, I'm guessing you'll say, as Methodist pastor James Moore once did in the title of one of his books, "Yes, Lord, I have sinned, but I have several excellent excuses." Are you ready?

You're eating out, and your waiter brings you the bill. You notice that the bill is less than it should have been. The waiter failed to charge you for your drinks or an entrée. Do you say anything? Restaurant margins are often fairly slim—net profits typically range from 2 percent to 6 percent.[1] If you and your friends have a hundred-dollar check at a full-service restaurant, and your waiter forgot to charge you for drinks or an entrée, if you don't say anything, the restaurant may have just lost all of the profit on your meal and you've consumed something you didn't pay for. This is a violation of the eighth commandment.

Let's talk about taxes. Many of you will read this book during Lent, and tax day usually falls close to the time of Easter. Have you ever overstated the value of your donations? Not reported all of your income? Have you been paid in cash and forgotten to report it as income? For as long as people have paid taxes, they've tried to find ways to avoid them. The most recent estimates are that tax evasion and fraud cost the U.S. government $450 billion in lost tax revenue every year. About one of every six dollars owed to the government is not paid by virtue of tax evasion. If you don't pay your share of your taxes, are you smart, or are you stealing from the government, from other taxpayers, or from our children, who somehow, one day, must make up the difference?

Have you ever sneaked into a second movie after watching the one you paid for? Have you borrowed things that you never gave back? Or used someone else's Netflix account to watch your favorite shows? In any of these scenarios, you have taken something you didn't pay for.

Have you traded in a car or, worse, sold it without revealing its problems to the new owner or the dealership you traded it to? Is that not a form of stealing too? Or dinged someone's door without leaving a note? Have you taken credit for someone else's work? It's possible to steal even something like praise or affirmation or credit.

It's possible that I've not yet found your violation of the eighth commandment. LaVon and I try to disclose everything we know about anything we sell. We don't "borrow" anyone's Netflix. We report all of our income and pay our share of taxes. We're not doing any of these things above, and I'm guessing that may be true for most of you. So let me try one more example of theft, which my friend Rabbi Art Nemitoff suggested when he and I discussed the commandments. (My friend can be a bit irritating sometimes, as I've found is the case with a good rabbi!)

Art suggested that every time we are late for a meeting, every time someone else has to wait for us, we are stealing *time* from them. Art's words hit me like an arrow to the heart. Time, for many people, is the most valuable thing they possess. It is more valuable to them than money. Yet, knowing this, I am still routinely late for *everything*. In fact, I was late just this morning for a haircut.

Let's play that out a bit. My being five minutes late for my haircut meant that Holly, the woman who cuts my hair, was now five minutes behind. She had another appointment ten minutes after mine, and instead of having a ten-minute break (during which time she also had to clean up her station) she now had five minutes—no time even to sit down and rest for a minute, use the restroom, or get a drink of water. I just stole that time from her. She was gracious as I walked in—she's used to my showing up five minutes late whenever she cuts my hair. But thanks to Rabbi Art, I now feel a conviction about this act and am working to correct it.

Here's the point: We're all thieves, even you.

The Worth of One's Labor

We've all violated the eighth commandment, and God is calling us to stop stealing. But I also think scripture extends this command beyond our individual actions, prohibiting practices that might be widespread or even approved of in society. In fact, many scholars believe that the prohibition against stealing was largely about stealing people—kidnapping and enslaving them.

Slavery was an accepted practice in every ancient culture. And despite having been liberated from slavery themselves, the ancient Israelites continued to practice it. Israelites could sell themselves into slavery to satisfy their debts or sell their children into slavery for similar reasons. Foreigners conquered in war could be forced into slavery too. There are more than two hundred verses in the Bible that seem to accept slavery as a fact of life. They are a reminder that even the biblical authors, to borrow the language Paul uses in 1 Corinthians 13:12, saw "through a glass dimly." Their ethics were shaped by their faith, but also by the context in which they lived. That historical context made it difficult for the biblical authors to imagine a world without slavery.

Israelites were, however, required to place limits around the practice of slavery, at least for their fellow Israelites who were their slaves. There were limits on the punishment of slaves. There was a time limit placed on the period of ownership of an Israelite slave (six years, though foreign slaves could be owned in perpetuity). A slave could be redeemed, their freedom purchased by family or friends. And to the point of the eighth commandment, Israelites were not to kidnap a fellow Israelite and force them into slavery or steal them to sell them to another as a slave. This applied not only to males but also to women, who were sometimes purchased as wives for the slave owner or his sons.

The penalty was harsh if you broke this rule. Deuteronomy 24:7 says, "If someone is caught kidnapping [stealing] their fellow Israelites, intending to enslave the Israelite or sell them, that kidnapper must die. Remove such evil from your community!" The same Hebrew word that is translated in the eighth commandment as "steal" is in these two verses translated as "kidnap."

Today we call this practice of stealing people and forcing them into slavery human trafficking. This sometimes involves abducting people but can also mean recruiting people through deception, threat, or other form of coercion to perform involuntary labor. We often hear of human trafficking in the sex trade, and that represents the majority of cases brought to trial in the United States. But trafficking may also include work in other fields—agriculture, manufacturing, domestic service, hospitality—and, in some parts of the world, abducting or coercing children to fight in war.

The eighth commandment clearly applies to human trafficking. It also applies to exploiting workers by withholding wages or paying employees a substandard wage. This is what James refers to in his epistle when he writes,

> Pay attention, you wealthy people! . . . Consider the treasure you have hoarded in the last days. Listen! Hear the cries of the wages of your field hands. These are the wages you stole from those who harvested your fields. The cries of the harvesters have reached the ears of the Lord of heavenly forces. You have lived a self-satisfying life on this earth, a life of luxury. You have stuffed your hearts in preparation for the day of slaughter. (James 5:1–5)

James's epistle was written to Christians. Were these words written to members of the Christian communities who were exploiting people or about people who exploited the members of the church? Perhaps both. Throughout scripture we find warnings of God's anger toward those who enrich themselves by not fairly compensating the workers in their fields or by taking advantage of the poor. The "market" may make it possible to pay someone a subsistence wage, but the biblical idea of justice would call a Christian to ask if the wages being paid are fair, reflect the real value of the labor, and provide a living wage. The commandment may lead us to ask if the compensation we're providing, and the relative compensation of our employees, is fair and just.

Years ago, one of my parishioners, a man named John, was the vice president of a company in Kansas City that was experiencing a downturn in its business. As the executive team met and discussed their options, the talk turned to letting employees go. The company was not large; I seem to recall they had a few dozen employees. John spoke up and proposed that if each of the executive team members took a pay cut, they would not have to let anyone go for a while, hopefully weathering the storm. When the executive team rejected the idea, he resigned, asking them to use his compensation to retain for a couple more months the employees they had been planning to release.

When businesses were forced to close during the coronavirus pandemic, I spoke with a number of senior leaders of companies in Kansas City who were forgoing their salaries as they continued to pay their employees even when the business was shut down. These were men and women who had already been serious about fair compensation for their employees.

Most of us are not senior leaders in companies, but we all have employees—people who work for us—or people who serve us, even if we don't think of them as our employees. When the coronavirus pandemic hit, one of the members of our church, Lyn, had been a waitress for forty-one years. She had worked at Denny's for the last ten. When the restaurant was forced to close, she lost her source of income.

A week later, the men from a Bible study that met once a week at her Denny's called the restaurant, asking how they could reach Lyn. They had a gift for her, they said. These guys had taken up an offering to cover the tips they would have paid her, plus more for the time she would be unemployed. She was in tears as she told me this. It was a picture of a group of guys thinking about the people who served them, concerned for the vulnerable, and doing something to help.

I'm guessing you can think of people you went out of your way to encourage or to care for during this time as well. That's the heart of the eighth command—a habit of seeking to care for and bless those around us. As we've seen throughout our study of the Ten Commandments, on the back side of every "thou shalt not" is a life-giving "thou shalt." That's what these guys were practicing as they sought to care for Lyn, who for years had waited on and served them.

Jesus and the Eighth Commandment

That takes us to Jesus. In his meeting with the rich young ruler, Jesus cites the eighth commandment as an essential practice for inheriting eternal life (Matthew 19:18, Mark 10:19, and Luke 18:20). Do not steal. But then Jesus calls the wealthy young man to give what he has to the poor. For Jesus the command was not just to avoid taking but pointed to a greater principle of loving one's neighbor: the effort to bless and care for others. It was a rhythm of compassion and generosity Jesus calls us to.

As I wrote earlier, Jesus's Golden Rule in Matthew 7:12

may be the greatest antidote to our struggle with stealing: "Do unto others as you would have them do unto you." This is such a simple guide. Would I want others to let me know if I undercharged them? "Do unto others . . ." Would I want others to ding my door without saying anything? "Do unto others . . ." Would I want to be taken advantage of by my employer? Or have credit taken for something I'd worked hard on? How would I feel about someone stealing my time by being perennially late? "Do unto others . . ." When you're not sure if what you are about to do is stealing or otherwise unethical, run it through the Golden Rule test. Would I want someone to do this to me?

There's a second antidote to stealing found in the teachings of Jesus and throughout scripture. We'll focus on it more in the final chapter of this book, but it is important to mention here as well. If stealing is about taking what isn't yours (time, money, property, even things like accolades), its antidote would be giving what you have to those who have no right to expect it. Again and again in scripture, we're commanded to give—particularly to the poor and to those who need what we have. Proverbs 22:9 captures it well: "Happy are generous people, because they give some of their food to the poor." And Jesus, who speaks about generosity as a primary virtue of the Christian life, evokes it in one of his most powerful parables: the parable of the sheep and the goats. Here he describes what will happen at the final judgment of the world:

> Then the king will say to those on his right, "Come, you who will receive good things from my Father. Inherit the kingdom that was prepared for you before the world began. I was hungry and you gave me food to eat. I was

> thirsty and you gave me a drink. I was a stranger and you
> welcomed me. I was naked and you gave me clothes to
> wear. I was sick and you took care of me. I was in prison
> and you visited me." (Matthew 25:34–36)

The blessed in the Kingdom of Heaven will be those who *gave,* whether it was drink, a warm welcome, clothing, or care.

Jesus regularly warned his disciples about the lure of wealth and possessions—the motivation behind much stealing: "Watch out! Guard yourself against all kinds of greed. After all, one's life isn't determined by one's possessions, even when someone is very wealthy" (Luke 12:15). "Stop collecting treasures for your own benefit on earth, where moth and rust eat them and where thieves break in and steal them. Instead, collect treasures for yourselves in heaven, where moth and rust don't eat them and where thieves don't break in and steal them. Where your treasure is, there your heart will be also" (Matthew 6:19–21).

Generosity, not greed or desire, is meant to be our way of life. This means generosity not only with our resources but also with our praise, with giving credit, with our desire to bless others, with our faithfulness to God. We are not meant to steal or take; instead we are meant to give and share.

At the peak of the coronavirus epidemic, I stood in front of our church as people drove up with groceries in their trunks that they had purchased for people in Kansas City who were struggling. It was thirty degrees and raining, the rain freezing on the cars and trees. Yet five women were busily collecting the groceries and thanking each of the hundred drivers who stopped by that morning for their selfless acts. I walked into the church to find women who were preparing medical-grade fabric with instructions so that our members could make fifteen thousand masks at a time when our hospitals were nearly out. Meanwhile, a doctor was helping volunteers convert fifty gallons of 190-proof alcohol into hand sanitizer for homeless shelters that couldn't find sanitizer in our city. And this was just a fraction of what happened in that one twenty-four-hour day as people tried to give food, protective equipment, and, more than anything, encouragement. Here's what I noticed about all these volunteers: They all seemed joyful.

In life we're either givers or takers. But Jesus was right when he said, "It is more blessed to give than to receive." This is the life-giving back side of the eighth commandment. Don't steal, do give. They are two sides of the same coin.

Jesus, a Thief, and Us

Since we've learned in this chapter that we've all broken the eighth command, I can't end without mentioning the one Gospel story in which Jesus himself interacted with two convicted thieves. Whether we've engaged in outright theft or lived lives of complete generosity, I believe this story offers hope to us all.

Matthew and Mark tell us two thieves were crucified with Jesus, one on either side. The Greek word used for these two was *lestai,* which can signify not just a petty thief but a violent criminal (as well as a rebel). Luke uses the word *kakourgoi*—literally, "people who did bad things"—to describe them.

As Jesus hung on the cross, hearing the insults of those who crucified him, he prayed, "Father, forgive them, for they don't know what they're doing." One of the thieves, hearing this, started to mock Jesus. But the other spoke up for Jesus, defending him. Then he said to Jesus, "Jesus, remember me when you come into your kingdom." Jesus replied, "I assure you that today you will be with me in paradise" (Luke 23:42–43). I love this moment. At the end of his life, wracked with pain, Jesus forgives and offers eternal life to a thief.

I'm a thief. You're one too. I didn't realize how much of one I was until I really studied the eighth commandment. But I love the fact that, to the end, Jesus was still forgiving sinners. And the final sinner Jesus forgave before he died was a thief. *Kyrie eleison.* Lord, have mercy.

What Jesus Might Say to You

Your character is seen in the small things, and I see all the small things. I've seen every good and right and selfless act you've ever done. I've also seen the times you took what wasn't yours. As I forgave the thief on the cross that day when he asked for my mercy, I will forgive you. Don't forget, my child, that you'll find the deepest meaning and the greatest joy not by what you acquire but by what you give.

IX

Sticks, Stones, and the Power of Words

Do not testify falsely against your neighbor.

—Exodus 20:16

On June 28, 1984, Darryl Burton was arrested for the crime of murder. Thirty days earlier, a man named Donald had been shot and killed while filling his gas tank at a convenience store in St. Louis. Eyewitnesses identified the killer as a short (five-foot-six), light-skinned black man. Darryl is five foot ten, and his skin much darker than the description in the police report. Yet on the basis of two witnesses, and with only an hour-long meeting with his public defender before the trial, Darryl was convicted of murder. Darryl writes of his conviction:

> There was no motive, no fingerprint, no weapon, no DNA evidence, no confession, or any evidence connecting me to the crime. The only thing that connected me to the case were two lying eyewitnesses' snitch testimo-

nies. These two men testified falsely against me because
they were making deals with the police and prosecution
to have their serious criminal charges they were facing
dropped.[1]

Darryl's lawyer was, like many public defenders, responsible
for more cases than a defense attorney can reasonably handle.
An eyewitness to the murder attended the trial and told the
police, "You have the wrong man. That is not the man I saw
commit this crime." But Darryl's lawyer hadn't interviewed
her in preparation for the case, and she was not allowed to
testify. Darryl was sentenced to fifty years in prison, plus
twenty-five years to be served consecutively—meaning he
would spend at least seventy-five years in prison before becoming eligible for parole. All of this on the basis of two false
witnesses who stood to gain by testifying against him on behalf of the state. It would take twenty-four years—until Au-
gust 29, 2008—for Darryl Burton to be exonerated.[2]

It is estimated that somewhere between 1 and 4 percent of
persons currently incarcerated are falsely accused and wrong-
fully convicted. That means that prosecutors get it right 96 to
99 percent of the time. But given that 2.3 million people are
imprisoned in the United States today, the rate of wrongful
convictions means there are between 23,000 and 92,000 people languishing behind bars for crimes they did not commit.
We see in Darryl's story the devastating impact of false witnesses, particularly in a system where public defenders are
overworked and testimony can be suppressed.

It was this very kind of situation that the ninth commandment was meant to address.

False Witnesses in Criminal Cases

In the Torah, murder and adultery were punishable by death. So, too, were Sabbath breaking, idolatry, blasphemy, stealing (especially kidnapping), and certain forms of dishonoring one's parents. Even when crime was not punishable by death, the legal consequences were often severe.

The punishments were meant to serve as deterrents from crime and guardrails that helped maintain justice and righteousness within Israel's community. But a criminal justice system—and with it a just society—works only if people tell the truth in court. Bringing false accusations against an individual can have catastrophic consequences.

A well-known example is the story of King Ahab, Queen Jezebel, and a man named Naboth, found in 1 Kings 21. We read there that King Ahab desired to purchase a vineyard near the royal palace, a vineyard belonging to Naboth the Jezreelite. The king wanted to transform Naboth's vineyard into a vegetable garden for the palace, so he offered Naboth a fair price or an even better vineyard elsewhere. But Naboth was unwilling to sell his vineyard, for it had been in his family for some time. Under the law at the time, even the king could not force someone to sell their property if they did not wish to do so.

But the king was not used to being told no. He returned to the palace sullen. Jezebel, seeing her husband, said to him,

"Aren't you the one who rules Israel? Get up! Eat some food and cheer up. I'll get Naboth's vineyard for you myself." So she wrote letters in Ahab's name, putting his seal on them. She sent them to the elders and officials who lived in the same town as Naboth. This is what she wrote in the letters: "Announce a fast and place Naboth at the head of the people. Then bring in two liars in front of him and have them testify as follows: 'You cursed God and king!' Then take Naboth outside and stone him so he dies." (1 Kings 21:7–10)

And that is precisely what the elders did. They held a dinner to which Naboth was invited. False witnesses came and testified at the dinner that Naboth had cursed God and king, and the people stoned Naboth to death. After this, Ahab took Naboth's vineyard.

It is easy to see why the ninth commandment was so important. Even with the prohibition in place, there were plenty of people willing to lie if they knew they could get away with it.

Deuteronomy 17:6 notes, "Capital punishment must be decided by two or three witnesses. No one may be executed on the basis of only one testimony." This was meant to serve as a safeguard against false convictions. Further, the witnesses who testified against the one being put to death were required to be the first to stone the convicted individual when the death penalty was administered. It is thought that those putting the condemned to death stood on a platform above and dropped heavy stones upon their head or torso, crushing them to death. Being forced to drop the first stones was thought to be one more deterrent to keep persons from falsely testifying against their neighbor. But as was the case with Naboth (and Darryl), it was possible to find people who would testify against another if they had something to gain by it.

It is worth noting at this juncture that at the center of the Christian faith is a man who was convicted and put to death by the state as a result of false witnesses. Listen to these words from Matthew 26:59–61:

> The chief priests and the whole council were looking for false testimony against Jesus so that they could put him to death. They didn't find anything they could use from the many false witnesses who were willing to come forward. But finally they found two who said, "This man said, 'I can destroy God's temple and rebuild it in three days.'"

When Jesus spoke of destroying God's temple, he was referring to his own body and his coming death and resurrection. But upon the testimony of false witnesses who misconstrued his words, Jesus was put to death.

Naboth, Jesus, and Darryl Burton are all examples of the tragic consequences of a false witness and the reality that there are always people who are willing to give false testimony if it serves their own interests. False testimony in a courtroom is a crime—we call it perjury. But as we will see, the commandment not to bear false witness against others has application far beyond the courtroom. Ultimately, it is an antidote to the many ways our words can bring others pain.

Politics and the Ninth Commandment

We live in a time when it is increasingly difficult to tell what is true. In our nation and local communities, our traditional sources for investigating, discerning, and reporting the truth are caught in the political polarization that is dividing our country. Regardless of how fair and unbiased a media outlet

attempts to be, if its reports are critical of a politician or political party, they will be blasted by supporters of that party or
politician as "fake news." We tend to choose news sources
that align with or confirm our biases, which serves only to
deepen our national polarization.

This polarization sometimes manifests itself in people of
faith participating in bearing false witness in the area of politics. Because we've not taken the time to listen to or understand the political "other," we often represent them in ways
that do not, in fact, reflect their views. Rather than digging
in to understand another's views and then debating and discussing them, it is easier to oversimplify and misrepresent their
views.

When I've sat and actually listened to the views of someone with whom I strongly disagree, my own position has
often changed or softened. The conversation allows me to
understand some part of their argument that I haven't heard
before, or see the motivation behind their deeply held convictions. I might not agree with the other person by the end,
but I've often come to appreciate their perspective.

Absent that kind of listening and seeking to understand,
we're left listening only to our "side" of the political divide
and reciting news or positions that confirm our biases, which
serves to deepen the polarization. This is what often happens
on social media. Social media has many wonderful benefits.
But it can also be a vehicle for bearing false witness in the area
of politics and beyond.

For many young adults (and others), Facebook, Twitter,
and Instagram have replaced ABC, NBC, CBS, and Fox as
the major sources of news. In the 2016 presidential election
season, the Pew Center found that 23 percent of Americans
knowingly or unknowingly shared a made-up news story on

social media.[3] Nearly one in four of us was posting fabricated stories that aligned with our own biases about this or that candidate or party. This is another form of false testimony. When we publicly share something as fact that we have not verified as factual, I would suggest we are, perhaps unwittingly, violating the ninth commandment.

In the time before social media, people did much the same thing by forwarding "chain" emails. Often these would have fabricated stories and doctored photos about one's political adversaries aimed at inflaming the passions of people sympathetic to the sender's views. Near the bottom of these emails, there would be an encouragement to forward the message to others, leading the email to go viral.

During that time, I would occasionally have parishioners come to me after worship with one of these emails in hand, asking if I knew about the outrageous things a particular politician had said or done. The stories almost always seemed inaccurate and designed to inflame. I would encourage the person to visit a fact-checking website to verify whether the claim was accurate or not. These sites are intended to be non-partisan locations to verify or debunk stories and claims circulating on the Web.[4] Almost always, they would come back the next week to tell me they had found out the claim was not true, and thank me for suggesting they check it out. But while email chains like these have largely stopped, social networks like Facebook, Twitter, and Instagram have made it even easier to bear false witness.

I've known a couple dozen elected officials personally. Some were members of Congress. Others were governors, mayors, and people serving in various state and local offices. Nearly all of them were remarkable people of integrity, choosing to serve as public officials for considerably less money than they would have earned working in law or business. I did not always agree with all of their policy positions, but I was impressed by their motives, their ethics, and their service. They knew they would be criticized on the job, and most were prepared for this. What they were not always prepared for was the constant barrage of hateful speech, false accusations, and occasionally threats they were subjected to, at times from people who considered themselves Christians.

Having seen what happens to many people as they practice politics, I've wondered if politics might not be the true test of our character and faith. Can we practice politics while seeking always to tell the truth? Do we express love in the way we live out our political convictions? Are the fruits of the Spirit evident in our conversations and interactions with people whom we disagree with?

Every other year, there is a major election at the national level. Which means that as you read this chapter, we've either just completed an election or are preparing for one. I want to encourage you to remember this commandment and consciously decide not to share false testimony. People of faith should debate issues, ideas, and approaches to public policy. But let's not pass on as fact what is hearsay. Let's not be purveyors of fake news. Let's love our neighbor, including those on the other side of the political aisle, as we love ourselves.

Beyond Politics

Of course, it is not only in the realm of politics that we struggle with this commandment. In fact, more often the struggle against false witnessing takes place in our personal lives. It is so easy to gossip about another, to participate in backbiting, and to speak of others in unflattering or harmful ways.

We seem hardwired to share gossip. There is something within us that enjoys knowing the "latest dirt" or sharing the "inside story" on someone else. At the office, this used to take place around the water cooler. It was the stuff that was shared at the barbershop or beauty salon. An amazing amount of gossip happens in church groups, where it is sometimes shared as a "prayer concern." Gossip makes us feel empowered, often because it makes us feel morally superior as we point out the perceived failures or foibles of others or pass along what someone shared with us in confidence. In the process, we bring harm to people and damage their reputations.

Once again, social media has made this so much easier to do. In a Pew survey conducted in 2018, 32 percent of teens said that others had spread false rumors about them online. This was more prevalent among girls, 39 percent of whom reported false rumors spread about them online.[5]

But it's not just teenagers who struggle with gossip, rumormongering, and false testimony in using social media. I know Christian leaders who routinely vilify others, pass on innuendos about those with whom they disagree, and otherwise falsely testify through their posts on social media. I've been on the receiving end of these posts on more than a few occasions.

People can be terribly cruel with their words. They can post falsehoods and half-truths as facts online. And the results can be devastating. The apostle James writes of our tongue (and today he could include our fingers on a keyboard):

The tongue is a small flame of fire, a world of evil at work in us. It contaminates our entire lives. Because of it, the circle of life is set on fire. The tongue itself is set on fire by the flames of hell. People can tame and already have tamed every kind of animal, bird, reptile, and fish. No one can tame the tongue, though. It is a restless evil, full of deadly poison. With it we both bless the Lord and Father and curse human beings made in God's likeness. Blessing and cursing come from the same mouth. My brothers and sisters, it just shouldn't be this way! (James 3:6–10)

My aim is never to share, send, post, or speak words that misrepresent others, bear false witness about them, or otherwise harm them. I hope to speak or write only words that give grace to those who hear. Still, there are times I have said, shared, or posted things that violated these intentions. Here I am reminded of another verse from James: "Those who consider themselves religious and yet do not keep a tight rein on their tongues deceive themselves, and their religion is worthless" (James 1:26, NIV).

I mentioned in the opening of this book that I've violated every one of the Ten Commandments, when understood as Jesus read them. The same is true here. I've never falsely accused or testified about someone in court. But I have been guilty of gossip, of backbiting, of bearing false witness about another in conversations with friends. I would never consciously and intentionally lie about another, but I have undoubtedly passed on hearsay or speculation, or assumed the worst of others without actually having all the facts. I never wish or intend to do this, but I'm certain I've done it. The fact that Jesus and the apostles addressed this kind of talk so frequently tells me that the earliest Christians struggled with it too.

Again, social media makes this so easy to do. Several years ago, a pastor of another church posted something about me on social media that was factually untrue. The post questioned my integrity. Usually I don't respond to posts like this, but in this case I knew the person, and I sent him a private message explaining part of the story he did not know. He immediately sent a note back saying, "I'm so sorry, I didn't know that part of the story. I'm deleting my post." I was grateful for his apology, but the tweet had already been seen by who knows how many people. Deleting it could not take it back.

In the last few years, our pastors have officiated at the funerals of more than thirty people who took their own lives. Half were either members of our church or family of members. The other half were people who were loosely associated with our church or had no church family. For several of the young adults who took their lives, one contributing factor was hurtful things that were said to them or about them on social media. Each of these young people served as a clear reminder that, despite the rhyme our parents taught us as children—"Sticks and stones can break my bones, but words can never harm me"—words can, in fact, harm us.

Broader Still: Dishonesty

Leviticus 19:11–12 brings together both the technical meaning of the commandment and its broader application when it states, "You must not steal nor deceive nor lie to each other. You must not swear falsely by my name, desecrating your God's name in doing so; I am Yahweh." In essence, the meaning of the ninth commandment becomes "Do not lie."

Recently, a group of famous and well-heeled parents were caught in a web of deception, having paid significant sums of money to fabricate information about their children in order to see them accepted into prestigious universities. Top colleges admit a very small percentage of the students who apply. By means of their deceit, these parents of young adults had stolen admission spots that might have gone to others.

People were outraged by this story, but elsewhere in our society, we've become so used to deception that many now consider it a "negotiating skill." It's not uncommon to hear of people lying on their job applications. They report higher grades in college than they really had, or record more impressive past employment positions than the ones they actually held. It is not uncommon for businesses to promise clients something they know they cannot deliver, at least not on the schedule they've promised, in order to get the deal.

At times I wonder if we even realize we are lying. Perhaps we're just "stretching the truth." Or maybe we've repeated our lies so much that we've come to believe them. But our false testimony, our deception, has consequences—namely, that it often leads to injustice. In the case of business dealings, the client and her or his business suffers as a result of the deception. Lying on a résumé and in an interview may mean a better-qualified candidate did not get the job and the employer is hiring someone less qualified than they intended.

Several years ago, a woman whom I'll call Kelly[6] came to me ready to file for divorce. Her husband lied to her about everything, she said. This included small things, such as telling her he'd left work late when in truth he had stopped for a drink on the way home. He lied about how he spent money and what he spent it on. Sometimes he lied about really big things. He was a compulsive liar, and his lying was destroying her. She wept as she described her utter lack of trust in anything he said and the pain she felt, living with a man who didn't tell the truth. Their marriage ultimately did not survive the deceit.

Few things are more deadly to a marriage, friendship, or familial relationship than deceit. Relationships are built on trust and trust is built on honesty.

Yet the reality is that bearing false witness, or falsely testifying about ourselves and about others, is ubiquitous in our society. This is a moral crisis that undermines our institutions and our relationships. The ninth commandment was given because there was a basic recognition that a society cannot stand when false testimony becomes an acceptable practice.

Is It Ever Okay to Lie?

At times I've been asked if lying is always wrong. The answer is no. The commandment against bearing false witness is aimed at protecting one's neighbor from harm, but there are times when telling the truth might actually bring greater harm to another. These circumstances are rare. As a rule, we're not to lie or deceive. But sometimes the obligation to love our neighbor—particularly to avoid causing them harm—carries the greater weight.

Irena Sendler worked for the Social Welfare Department in Warsaw, Poland, during the Holocaust. A trained health-care worker, she volunteered to enter Warsaw's Jewish ghetto to treat those with typhus and other diseases. The Germans were little concerned for the Jewish residents but did not want to risk the spread of diseases to their guards. So they approved Irena's request and allowed her to enter.

Over a period of several years, Irena forged documents to help residents escape the ghetto. She helped smuggle people out to safety. She even carried babies out in the bags she used to carry her medical supplies. In total, she helped more than two thousand people escape the ghetto, including four hundred children. Frequently the Germans questioned her to see if she was aiding the escape of Jews. She always lied, and in doing so she practiced selfless and sacrificial love. For Irena, the command to love was more important than the command to not deceive. In fact, her act of deception was, in this case, an act of love.

Long before Irena Sendler's heroic acts, two midwives, Shiphrah and Puah, did something similar when Egypt's pharaoh ordered that baby boys born to Israelite women be put to death. The midwives refused, and word got out. When Pharaoh asked them why they were not obeying his orders, they lied. "Hebrew women aren't like Egyptian women," they explained. "They're much stronger and give birth before any midwives can get to them" (Exodus 1:19). As a result of their courage and deception in saving the Hebrew boys—including, presumably, the infant Moses—Exodus reports, "God treated the midwives well" (Exodus 1:20).

More recently, I think of a woman who was in a terrible automobile accident several years ago. The woman's daughter had died in the crash, and she herself was in the hospital, fighting for her life. When she asked her friends if her daughter was okay, her friends told her that her daughter was fine. They were concerned that if the woman knew of her daughter's death, the grief might kill her. They did not want to deceive her, but neither did they want to contribute to her death. As soon as the woman's condition was stable, they shared with her the news.

In each of these cases, deceit was deemed necessary to save another's life. The ethical duty to save a life was in conflict with the ethical duty to tell the truth. In cases in which the duty to save a life conflicts with the ethical duty to tell the truth, the duty to protect life outweighs the duty to tell the truth.

Again, cases like these are rare. More often our false testimony is not about protecting others from harm but about protecting ourselves, our self-esteem, and our approval from others. Other times we use false testimony about ourselves to deflect blame and avoid responsibility.

The ninth command calls us to integrity—to avoid claiming to be one kind of person while, in fact, being someone quite different. Jesus criticized the Pharisees for being "hypocrites," and he called his disciples to avoid practicing their religious devotion before others in order to win their approval: "Be careful that you don't practice your religion in front of people to draw their attention. If you do, you will have no reward from your Father who is in heaven" (Matthew 6:1). He went on to warn against showy prayers, bragging about one's giving to the poor, and fasting to be noticed by others. When our actions are done to impress others, rather than as an attempt to be the person God calls us to be, our actions may be a form of false testimony.

Here, once more, we find that the commandment speaks urgently to our lives today. I've never falsely testified against anyone in court, but I am a recovering hypocrite who regularly falls off the wagon and back into hypocrisy. With every sermon I preach, I am preaching to myself before I preach it to others. Even writing this book on the Ten Commandments, I recognize with each chapter ways in which the commandment convicts me.

Here I think it's important to consider another form of false testimony we make about ourselves—one that might not seem as obvious. This form of false testimony involves the *negative* things we tell ourselves: that we're worthless, ugly, stupid, or worse. I've known people for whom this kind of self-talk has led to self-harm. Here I'm reminded of John 8:44, where Jesus describes the devil as "a liar and the father of liars." When I counsel someone struggling with negative self-talk and thoughts of self-harm, I remind them of these words of Jesus and invite them to think of the devil himself as the source of these lies. When it comes to the devil's accusations, we are to resist and reject him in the name of Jesus Christ, who testified with his life that we have value and worth.

The devil seems equally gratified to puff you up with pride as to destroy you with feelings of worthlessness. Both are forms of false witness we make about ourselves.

Jesus on the Ninth Commandment

On many occasions, Jesus was the subject of harsh words and false witnesses. Out of jealousy, his opponents sought to belittle and denigrate him. On several occasions they even accused him of being demon possessed. Imagine that. Jesus, who Christians believe incarnated God, being accused of "having a demon"! From a Christian perspective, could there be a more tragic example of bearing false witness?

Jesus understood what it was to be misrepresented by others. Perhaps this is why he said,

> Don't judge, so that you won't be judged. You'll receive
> the same judgment you give. Whatever you deal out will
> be dealt out to you. Why do you see the splinter that's in
> your brother's or sister's eye, but don't notice the log in
> your own eye? How can you say to your brother or sister,
> "Let me take the splinter out of your eye," when there's a
> log in your eye? You deceive yourself! First take the log
> out of your eye, and then you'll see clearly to take the
> splinter out of your brother's or sister's eye. (Matthew
> 7:1–5)

The religious leaders—and likely even his own disciples—routinely judged others. Jesus saw the good in others, the potential in others. He looked upon them with compassion, not judgment. I think of the sinful woman, traditionally seen as a prostitute, who wept at Jesus's feet in Luke 7. He had compassion for her, showed her mercy, and saw her not as a prostitute but as a human being, dearly loved by God. I think, too, of the rich man who longed to have eternal life but who struggled with his possessions. Mark tells us, "Jesus looked at him carefully and loved him" (Mark 10:21). Jesus modeled for us how we're to look at others—to see them with love and compassion and resist assuming the worst of them.

I love how Paul speaks of this in Philippians 2. In that passage, he puts forth Jesus as the example of how we are to relate to others: "Don't do anything for selfish purposes, but with humility think of others as better than yourselves. Instead of each person watching out for their own good, watch out for what is better for others" (Philippians 2:3–5). He points out that Jesus, though he was in the form of God, humbled himself and became a servant.

The opposite of bearing false witness about ourselves, particularly of the prideful sort, is humility. The opposite of bearing false witness against others is to speak words that build others up, words that give grace to those who hear. It is pretty simple to ask, *Is what I'm saying about someone else what I would want them to say about me? Does it reflect love or only my need to tell some tantalizing bit of news or, worse, to make myself feel better by telling of some shortcoming of another? Would I say this if the person were standing here?*

I'd like to end with a story about the power of false witness, from the life of the sixteenth-century Italian saint Philip Neri. One day a woman came to Father Neri confessing that she struggled with the sin of gossip. He heard her confession but sensed she did not understand just how serious a sin this was. So he prescribed an unusual act of penance.

"Do you have a feather pillow?" he asked. She nodded. "I want you to take your pillow to the top of the church tower where we ring the bell. There I want you to rip open your pillow and to release its feathers, then return to me." She thought it a strange request but did what the priest asked. She took her favorite feather pillow to the top of the church tower, opened it with her scissors, and disgorged its feathers. These were promptly scattered with the wind. She then returned to the priest and said, "Father, I've done as you requested. Am I now forgiven?" To which he replied, "Not yet. Now take your pillowcase and go collect all the feathers, and then you will be forgiven."

The woman finally understood the point of the penance: Her rumors and gossip, like the feathers from her pillow, had spread far and wide, and it would be impossible to gather them back up. Today we would say they'd gone viral. These rumors and acts of gossip were, in many cases, false testimony against her neighbors.

That leads me back to Darryl Burton. He spent twenty-four years in prison because of two false witnesses, an over-worked defense attorney, and a prosecutor who suppressed the testimony that might have cleared him. But here's what is most remarkable about his story. Darryl forgave them all. After years of bitterness and hate, the Lord set him free, and he forgave them all.

While in prison, Darryl made a promise to God: If you get me out of here, I'll serve you for the rest of my life. True to his word, Darryl went to seminary after getting out of prison, and for the last six years I've had the privilege of working alongside him at the Church of the Resurrection, where he serves as one of our pastors of congregational care. I am honored to call him my friend.

You've no doubt been hurt by the words of others, by false testimony, rumors, or gossip that brought you pain. Me too. But here's what makes it possible for me to forgive others when they've done this to me: I realize that I've been guilty of doing the same thing to others across the course of my life. And there's a God who offers mercy to us all.

Our words are powerful. With them we can destroy or build up. The ninth commandment calls us not to do harm with our words, and Jesus and the early church compel us to use our words to bless, to build up, and to do good to others. By refraining from doing evil with our words, and positively using our words to do good, we literally speak *words of life*.

What Jesus Might Say to You

I know you've been hurt by words others have spoken. I have been hurt too. But with your words, be careful not to harm others. Don't say anything about another that you would not say if they were listening in. Be truthful, and be careful not to judge others. You don't know their hearts. Instead, use your words as instruments of healing, blessing, and love. As you build others up, you'll find your own heart is filled with joy.

X

Keeping Up with the Joneses

You shall not covet your neighbor's house; you
shall not covet your neighbor's wife, or male or
female slave, or ox, or donkey, or anything that
belongs to your neighbor.

—Exodus 20:17, NRSV

When John Betar died in the fall of 2018, he and his
wife, Ann, had been married nearly eighty-six years.
They were thought to be the longest-wedded couple in
America, and perhaps the longest married in the history of
our nation. John was 107 years old at the time of his death.
Ann's death followed seven months later at the age of 103.

Late in their lives, the couple were interviewed frequently
and asked what it takes to stay married for so long. Among
their responses: "Live within your means and be content."[1]

Contentment isn't always a virtue. Several years ago, I was
asked on a health survey if I was content with the amount of
exercise I was getting, which at the time was zero. Of course

I was content—I'd not been exercising for years! But that was something I should not have been content with. Often that's our challenge in life. We are content with the things we should be discontent with and discontent with the things we're meant to be content with.

We're not alone in this. While in Cairo, I visited the Egyptian Museum and walked through the treasures of King Tutankhamun. If a late date is assumed for Moses and the Exodus, King Tut, as he is often called, would have been a contemporary of Moses. He lived for only seventeen years, ruling from the time he was eight or nine until his death. He became a household name in 1922, when archaeologist Howard Carter found his nearly intact tomb.

If you go to Cairo and view the treasures left in the boy king's tomb for his use in the afterlife, it is clear that the Egyptian elites likely struggled with the same discontentment we moderns do today. A whopping 5,398 items were found in Tut's tomb, including his solid-gold coffin, six chariots (think gold-plated ancient Ferraris), multiple gold-plated couches and chairs, a fabulous collection of jewelry, gold-covered chairs, clothes made from the finest linens, thirty jars of wine, and a great deal more. In the time of Moses, the wealthiest people in Egyptian society struggled with covetousness—the persistent craving for more, particularly what others have—in much the same way we do today.

When John Betar spoke about contentment as a key to remaining married over eighty years, he was talking about his and Ann's contentment with their material possessions (and hence their ability to live within their means). But I suspect he was also speaking about their decision to be content with each other. In this they were living the tenth commandment, which calls us to avoid coveting and taking another's mate.

The first commandment and the tenth form a bracket: Both deal with the human heart, but from different angles. In the first commandment, we're told to have no other gods before God. The last commandment deals directly with those "other gods" humans have always tended to worship—the material possessions and even people we are prone to covet. In many ways coveting is often the motivation behind our violation of all of the commandments. Coveting can be a form of idolatry. It can lead us to misuse God's name or work on the Sabbath or dishonor our parents. It is sometimes behind the violence we do to one another and is, by definition, central to adultery and stealing—in both of these last two commandments, coveting leads us to take what is not ours. In a sense, even bearing false witness can be the result of a heart that craves attention or vengeance or a host of other things that can lead us to hurt others by falsely testifying about them.

In this, our concluding chapter, we'll consider what covetousness is and why it's unhealthy for us. Then we'll look at three antidotes, taught by Jesus, intended to help us find contentment and fulfillment.

Ninth and Tenth Commandments?

We learned in the first chapter that Jews and various Christians have different ways of numbering the Ten Commandments. Just as this affects how people of different faiths divide the first and second commands, it also affects the ninth and tenth.

Catholics and Lutherans find two commandments in the prohibition against coveting. To do this, they turn to Deuteronomy's version of the last of the commandments, which, unlike the version in Exodus, places the prohibition against coveting your neighbor's wife on its own:

> IX. You shall not covet your neighbor's wife.
>   X. You shall not set your desire on your neighbor's house or land, his male or female servant, his ox or donkey, or anything that belongs to your neighbor. (Deuteronomy 5:21, NIV)

Notice once more that the commandments address only men. Men are not to covet their neighbor's wife, but women are not addressed. When you turn to the version of these prohibitions in Exodus 20:17 (NIV), it is made even more clear that the wife is the property of the husband, alongside the rest of the things he owns:

> X. You shall not covet your neighbor's house; you shall not covet your neighbor's wife, or male or female slave, or ox, or donkey, or anything that belongs to your neighbor.

This is the version that led Jews, the Eastern Orthodox Church, and most Protestant Christians to count all of this as one commandment—we are not to covet our neighbor's house, which includes wife, slaves, animals, and everything else.

The mention of wives and slaves as part of one's neighbor's house (that is, his property) once again raises questions for us. What are we to do with the fact that the Ten Commandments, this summation of the Law of Moses, counts wives as property and allows Israelites to own their family and other human beings?

When we read the scripture, part of the task of interpreting is, as we've seen at various places in our study, teasing out the cultural and historical context and distinguishing it from the timeless truth of God. The tenth command emerged during a time when people saw wives as part of the possessions of a husband. That same world also permitted the ownership of humans as slaves. The commands come to us through people living in a particular time and place, hearing the word of God in their own cultural and historical context.

In this command, I believe we must set aside the patriarchy in favor of the mutual partnership of Genesis 1. And we can read this command, and its mention of slavery, in the light of God's central redemptive work in Exodus: liberating slaves. By looking at these two ideas of patriarchy and slavery in the Ten Commandments in the light of Genesis 1 and Exodus 4:7–8, I believe we can conclude that patriarchy and slavery were not God's will but a part of the ancient Near Eastern culture in the late Bronze Age. With that background in mind, let's turn our focus to the point of this command: *Do not covet.*

This final command speaks profoundly to the human condition. It describes a fundamental struggle we all wrestle with: *our desire for what we do not, cannot, or should not have,* particularly when that thing belongs to another. The prohibition against coveting, like the other commandments, serves as a guardrail given by God to protect us and a guidepost to help us experience the good and beautiful life God intends.

The Nature of Desire

The Hebrew word translated as "covet" in Exodus 20:17 is *chamad*. It typically means to strongly desire something, but it often carries the sense of desiring something so much that you will do anything to have it. Hence the Common English Bible translates it not as "covet" but as "desire and try to take."

In the tenth commandment, as found in Deuteronomy 5:21, *chamad* is used in the first line, "Do not covet your neighbor's wife." But another word, *avah,* is used in the next line, "You shall not set your desire on your neighbor's house or anything that belongs to your neighbor." *Chamad* and *avah* can be used interchangeably, but often *avah* is used to signify a sense of craving. So the second part of the command in Deuteronomy might read, "Don't crave your neighbor's house or land, their male or female servants, their ox or donkey, or anything else that belongs to your neighbor."

Can you think of a time when you craved something that belonged to someone else? Or when you desired it so much you tried to take it? Watch little children at play, and you'll find this happening. One child begins to play with a toy, and another child yanks it out of the first child's hands, often exclaiming, "Mine!" Clearly the impulse to covet starts very early.

We saw glimpses of the sin of covetousness in previous chapters; first when David craved Uriah's beautiful wife, Bathsheba, and took her, and second when Jezebel and Ahab had Naboth killed so they could seize his vineyard. But we find the first record of the sin of covetousness in the story of Adam and Eve and their desire for Eden's forbidden fruit.

Chamad first appears in the Bible in Genesis 2 and 3, where we read of God planting a garden and placing within it the first man and the first woman. God gave the couple all of the fruit-bearing trees to eat from. Their fruit is described as "desirable" or "pleasing," a form of the Hebrew word *chamad*. But while Adam and Eve could eat of the fruit of nearly any tree they wished, there was one tree God had forbidden them to eat from: the tree of the knowledge of good and evil.

What happens when you are told you cannot have something? For many of us, it makes the object all the more enticing or desirable. If the speed limit is sixty-five, I find myself needing to drive seventy, or even seventy-five. If a sign says "Do not touch," it elicits from me an intense desire to touch the thing, even though I might not otherwise have thought of touching it. And when I'm told I can't have something, I find I want it all the more. This is what I think Paul had in mind when he wrote:

> I would not have known what it is to covet if the law had not said, "You shall not covet." But sin, seizing an opportunity in the commandment, produced in me all kinds of covetousness. (Romans 7:7b–8, NRSV)

This is what happened to Adam and Eve. Told they could not eat from the tree of the knowledge of good and evil, they began to desire—*chamad*—and covet this one tree.

In the Garden, a talking serpent (the tempter) speaks to Eve. He helps her rationalize why although God has forbidden her and Adam from eating from the tree, it is really okay. I picture Eve approaching the tree, touching its fruit, smelling it, pondering it, and listening to the serpent's quite reasonable explanations. All before finally plucking the fruit and eating it and encouraging Adam to do the same. In her exchanges with the snake, we see a sin before the sin of eating the forbidden fruit. It was a sin of the heart, in which Adam and Eve desired what was not theirs to take.

The story of Adam and Eve eating the forbidden fruit is among the most important in the Bible. Its purpose is not to tell us ancient history, nor to tell us whether woman or man brought sin into the world. It is meant to teach us about ourselves. We, like Adam and Eve, know there are things that are off-limits, things God says we should not have. But the very fact that they are forbidden piques our desire. We've all heard the serpent rationalize with us—that voice in our heads or the voices of others, attempting to convince us it's our right to have what we should not have—until finally we pick the forbidden fruit and eat it. As with Adam and Eve, the result is often shame, alienation, and guilt.

Adam and Eve were subsequently banished from paradise. As John Milton put it in the title of his famous work, paradise was "lost." And that's exactly what happens when we fall into covetousness in our own lives. I've known people who ended up in prison because they succumbed to their desire for some kind of forbidden fruit—the desire for wealth or power leading to white-collar crimes or the desire for a forbidden pleasure leading to jail time for prostitution or drug use. In each case, the person could recount the process of rationalization that led to their sin. They knew how it felt to have a conversation in their minds with the serpent. They felt the desire growing stronger and stronger for that which they were not meant to have.

Covetousness is often the deeper motivation behind our

violation of the other nine commands. In a sense, as we've seen, the tenth commandment addresses the heart of the Ten Commandments and serves as a recapitulation of them all.

Covetousness in the New Testament

The New Testament was written in Greek, not Hebrew. In Greek, there are several words that are used to describe coveting, and they highlight some of the different ways this command touches our lives. For example, one of these words is *pleonexia*. *Pleonexia* is a compound of two Greek words: *pleion*, which means "more," and *exo*, which means "to have." *Pleonexia*, in short, is the insatiable desire for more. It is sometimes translated as "covetousness," sometimes as "avarice," and often as "greed."

In Luke 12:15 (NRSV), Jesus said, "Be on your guard against all kinds of greed; for one's life does not consist in the abundance of possessions." The word translated as "greed" here is *pleonexia*. It describes a craving for more, based upon a false premise—a lie—that your life really *does* consist in the abundance of your possessions. Even among the first-century Jewish peasants to whom Jesus was speaking, greed or covetousness must have been a very real struggle.

Most Americans struggle with *pleonexia* as well. We live in an economic system that relies on fueling our desire for more to increase consumer spending. Those who manufacture, sell, or provide goods and services must constantly create new or improved products in order to persuade you to buy. It's not hard. Our hearts are so easily drawn to covet. Capitalism is a brilliant system in so many ways. It fuels innovation and constant improvement. It creates jobs and opportunities. But it also requires that thousands of companies, and tens of thousands of very smart people, work constantly to convince you that what you have is not enough. Marketers and advertisers are skilled at helping us see that if we had just a little "nicer" or "newer" or "bigger" or "better," we'd be happier and more fulfilled. Producers of goods and services must create discontent with what we have, thus fueling our desire for more.

On a shelf in my office, I keep a collection of all the cellphones I've owned. Sadly, the collection is missing my first four phones, which included a "bag phone" and three different "flip phones." But it does include each of the four versions of Apple's iPhone that I've purchased over the last thirteen years. Bear in mind, all four of these phones worked perfectly when I bought the next, more expensive version. But each new iPhone model was packed with new features that I convinced myself I had to have. (It is interesting how at first smaller was better, and now bigger is better. The same people who told me it was cool to have a small phone have convinced me that now I have to have one with a giant screen!)

Marketing is the task of making us aware of and convincing us that we need what someone else is selling. We're constantly being targeted with marketing. Every time I search for something online, Google takes note. It knows where I live, my gender, my preferences, and my age and stage in life. Facebook and Twitter do this as well. Each has an algorithm that helps the company serve me the ads that are most likely to appeal to me. Sometimes they're right, and sometimes it's a miss. Google seems to think I need hearing aids (hey, Google, my hearing is fine!). Facebook believes I'm interested in a new bed, pillows, or sheets (not sure why, but now that I think about it, new pillows sound nice). Twitter is offering me car insurance (thanks, Twitter, but I'm happy with my agent).

There's nothing wrong with all of this marketing. It's how Google, Facebook, and Twitter pay the bills. But it points to the truth that we live in a time when we're constantly encouraged to want more. Wanting things and shopping for them are not necessarily signs of covetousness. But when my passion for consuming consumes me—my time, my emotional and spiritual energy, or money that I should have spent on something else, when it becomes an obsession or a desire for something I'm not meant to have—it can cross the line into covetousness or greed.

Jesus describes our struggle with greed in the parable of the sower (sometimes more aptly called the parable of soils). In the story, he compares the Kingdom of God to a farmer planting seeds. As the farmer scattered his seeds, some fell on the hard path, where they could not grow and were eaten by birds. Some fell on shallow soil and sprang up quickly. But because the roots couldn't go deep into the soil, the plants shriveled when the sun started to beat down. Yet another group of seeds fell among the thorny plants. They began to grow, but the weeds choked out the seedlings. Finally, some seeds fell on the good soil, and they produced a harvest thirty, sixty, and one hundred times what was planted.

Jesus explains that the seeds represent God's message, which Jesus has been preaching. The soils represent human hearts and their receptivity to God's message. Notice particularly the seeds that fell among the thorny plants. Jesus notes:

> As for the seed that was spread among thorny plants, this
> refers to those who hear the word, but the worries of this

life and *the false appeal of wealth* choke the word, and it
bears no fruit. (Matthew 13:22, emphasis added)

Elsewhere Jesus tells his followers:

No household servant can serve two masters. Either you
will hate the one and love the other, or you will be loyal
to the one and have contempt for the other. You cannot
serve God and wealth. (Luke 16:13)

It's actually surprising just how often Jesus speaks about
money and our desire for more in the Gospels. And how relevant these passages are for us today. At fifty-six, LaVon and I
have been investing money in the stock market for over thirty
years. Apple stock we paid a few dollars per share for is now
trading for nearly $400 per share (likely higher as you read this
book!).[2] How easy it is to get caught up in the market and to
base my sense of happiness and security on how well the market is doing. The fact that Apple's logo is an apple with a bite
out of it is a reminder, at least to me, of Eve and Adam's struggle with covetousness and the serpent's suggestion that they
might finally be happy if they just had a bite of the forbidden
fruit.

Once more, I have to remember what Jesus so plainly said:
"One's life does not consist in the abundance of possessions,"
because there are voices constantly telling me that my life
might just consist in the things I own.

This theme is found throughout the New Testament. Paul
says it this way in 1 Timothy 6:9–10 (NRSV):

Those who want to be rich fall into temptation and are
trapped by many senseless and harmful desires that plunge

people into ruin and destruction. For the love of money is a root of all kinds of evil, and in their eagerness to be rich some have wandered away from the faith and pierced themselves with many pains.

These and other passages in the Gospels serve as Jesus's warning against the inordinate desire or craving for wealth and about how easily this chokes out the work of God in our lives and leads us away from the good life God intends for us.

My great-grandparents lived simpler lives, but they still knew craving. They did not have Amazon and other online retailers, but they had the Sears, Roebuck and Penny's catalogs. They would thumb through the pages, imagining what life would be like if only they had the things they saw in the catalog. But while they might have had desire, what they didn't have was credit cards and liberal access to debt to "buy now and pay later." Today we can do just that. We can purchase things on plastic and not feel any pain until the bill arrives.

Rising levels of debt are a sign of our struggle to finance the good life as it's regularly sold to us. In 2019 the average U.S. household was carrying $8,512 in credit card debt.[3] The average car loan has lengthened from thirty-six months to sixty-nine months over the last five decades.[4] There are many reasons we go into debt, but often it is the result of our discontent, our desire for more, and our unwillingness to live within our means. (Contrast this with the wisdom the Betars shared at the beginning of this chapter.) Twenty-six million Americans were unemployed at the peak of the pandemic; some of these were already only two to three paychecks away from financial disaster. Our financial problems can strain our relationships while diminishing our quality of life and ability to live as God's people. In the scriptures on the previous three pages, this is what Jesus and Paul were trying to say.

Early in our marriage, LaVon and I lived paycheck to paycheck. We knew well the stress I've just described. Today we don't live that way anymore. We don't carry revolving credit card debt. We hold on to our cars longer and pay them off earlier.

For Americans who are middle to upper-middle income and beyond, there is the temptation to spend money on things that don't satisfy. We buy clothes we don't need and often don't wear. We are sometimes careless with our money, forgetting that every dollar we spend on something that doesn't matter is a dollar we won't be able to use for something that does matter. We acquire more and more stuff, then rent storage units to hold it all. (In recent years, spending on the construction of storage facilities has increased fivefold.) Within days, or even moments, after we buy these things, we discover that they don't make us happy.

I can think of countless examples from my own life. In my garage, there's a 2002 Yamaha Road Star motorcycle that I put two hundred miles on last year. There's also a fabulous Meade LX90 telescope that I spent two thousand dollars on, only to see it now covered in dust. In my basement "man cave," I've got some impressive old baseball cards—a Babe Ruth, rookie cards for Satchel Paige and Jackie Robinson, several Mickey Mantles, and the complete Topps collection from 1964, the year I was born. I spent a year looking for the 1964 cards. Do you know how often I get these cards out to look at them, cards I must have spent hours collecting on eBay? Never. I'm reminded of the words of Isaiah 55:2: "Why spend money for what isn't food, and your earnings for what doesn't satisfy?" It is a question Isaiah could easily ask us today.

Again, not all desire is unhealthy or sinful. The scriptures speak repeatedly about God giving us the "desires of your heart." I think of the many meaningful things I desire—good food, the company of friends, the embrace of my wife, time with my children and granddaughter, a great meal shared with people I love, two weeks on a beach to read and walk and pray, a long and healthy life for me and my wife and family.

I don't believe any of these desires, including the baseball cards I never look at, reflected coveting, though some were simply not satisfying. So when does desire become coveting and a violation of the tenth commandment? Here are a few rules of thumb:

- When we desire something to the point that we would act immorally to take it from someone else, we have violated the tenth commandment.
- When we crave and become fixated on having something we're not meant to have, something that will hurt us or others, or something that God has said we're not to have, we violate the tenth commandment.
- When the object we desire becomes a false god or an idol (that which is more important to us than God), we violate the tenth commandment.
- When we've overspent, putting ourselves in debt in order to have what our heart craves, or when our spending keeps us from caring for our family or serving God, we've likely violated the tenth commandment.

The commandment not to covet was given to us by a God who cares about the state of our heart. When covetousness becomes our way of life, we find that, as Mick Jagger sang, we "can't get no satisfaction"—though we try and we try and we try and we try.

Where Satisfaction Is Found

Let's return to the question God asked in Isaiah 55:2: "Why spend money for what isn't food, and your earnings for what doesn't satisfy?" In the rest of that powerful passage, God beckons his people to pursue that which really does satisfy. And what is that? It is God himself and his covenant relationship with his people. God likens his covenant love to pure waters, to wine and milk and rich food. Then God continues,

> Seek Yahweh while he may be found,
>   call upon him while he is near;
> let the wicked forsake their way,
>   and the unrighteous their thoughts;
> let them return to Yahweh, that he may have mercy
>   on them,
>   and to our God, for he will abundantly pardon . . .
> [then] you shall go out in joy,
>   and be led back in peace;
> the mountains and the hills before you
>   shall burst into song,
> and all the trees of the field shall clap their hands
>   (Isaiah 55:6–7,12, NRSV)

It is when we return to our desire for God—to know God, to love him, to serve him, to belong to him—that we find our deepest satisfaction. Saint Augustine famously said it this way: "Thou hast made us for thyself, O Lord, and our heart is restless until it finds rest in thee."[5]

This is why the Ten Commandments begin with "I am Yahweh your God. . . . You must have no other gods before me. . . . Do not make an idol for yourself." The good and beautiful life cannot be found apart from God. And the more we make the things we crave our gods, the less joy and satisfaction we'll find in life. I've known people who had riches and power, fabulous vacations and country club memberships, but still felt empty inside. They learned from experience that real life was not found in the abundance of possessions.

Once more we turn to the words of Jesus in the Sermon on the Mount. "Don't worry about your life, what you'll eat or what you'll drink, or about your body, what you'll wear. Isn't life more than food and the body more than clothes? . . . Instead, desire first and foremost God's kingdom and God's righteousness, and all these things will be given to you as well" (Matthew 6:25,33). *First and foremost.* If we're meant to crave anything, it's the experience of knowing God, following Jesus, and pursuing God's will. This is where our deepest satisfaction will be found.

Paul, writing from a prison cell while awaiting the outcome of a trial that would determine if he would live or die, said this to the church at Philippi:

> I know the experience of being in need and of having more than enough; I have learned the secret to being content in any and every circumstance, whether full or

212 Words of Life

hungry or whether having plenty or being poor. I can
endure all these things through the power of the one who
gives me strength. (Philippians 4:12–13)

We might not be beaten or thrown into prison like Paul, but
the answer to our discomforts and discontent is the same.
Contentment, Paul writes, was found in his faith and trust in
Christ.

Antidotes to Coveting

I began this chapter by noting that contentment is the opposite of covetousness. But how do we cultivate it, or make
it more than a simple feeling that comes and goes? I'd like
to end by suggesting three practices that can help us escape the pull of inappropriate, misdirected, and overactive
desires.

Gratitude

Several years ago, I asked our congregation to keep a gratitude journal every day for a month. We gave them small
pocket journals that they could use to write two or three
things they were happy for each day. I kept one myself. For
many of our people, it was a transformational experience.
The simple act of recounting their blessings actually improved
their sense of well-being and satisfaction in life, even though
their circumstances remained the same.

Gratitude is a key to contentment and an antidote for coveting. I've noted elsewhere that the most basic form of prayer
and worship is just two words: *thank you.*[6] Scripture instructs

us to "give thanks to Yahweh, for he is good" (Psalms 107:1, 118:1, and 136:1, NRSV) and to "Give thanks in every situation because this is God's will for you in Christ Jesus" (1 Thessalonians 5:18). There's a wisdom to verses like these. The more I give thanks for what I have, the less I want what I don't have. This is true when it comes to stuff, jobs, even mates. Several times each day, I give thanks for my wife. I try to express gratitude to her again and again. The more I express my gratitude for her and to her, the less likely I am to covet someone else's wife. How could I, when I'm so grateful for LaVon?

Dozens of studies have been conducted on the power of gratitude. They've found that gratitude in marriage strengthens marriages. Gratitude expressed to employees makes for happier employees. Grateful kids are happier kids. Gratitude is a key to releasing our hearts from the power of desire. The more grateful I am for what I have, the less I feel the need for more.

Generosity

The second key to contentment is generosity, a virtue we considered in chapter 8. There is something about the act of giving that shakes us loose from craving's grasp. It is hard to focus on what you desperately want when you are busy giving to others. And we often find that the joy of giving far exceeds the joy of receiving, which is precisely what Jesus said: "It is more blessed to give than to receive" (Acts 20:35). The writer of Proverbs says something similar: "Generous persons will prosper; those who refresh others will themselves be refreshed" (Proverbs 11:25).

Today researchers in the fields of philanthropy and positive psychology are constantly "discovering" what the Bible has taught all along. Dr. Summer Allen, a researcher at the University of California at Berkeley focused on happiness, summarized some of the findings with these words:

> Can money buy happiness? It depends on what you spend it on. A survey of 632 Americans found that spending money *on other people* was associated with significantly greater happiness, regardless of income, whereas there was *no association* between spending on oneself and happiness.[7] (emphasis added)

I see this all the time in the congregation I serve. The happiest people I know are not necessarily the richest, but they are the most generous. I have heard hundreds of stories of amazing generosity, but many of my favorites are those that come from children. Here's one example, shared with me by the mother of a girl in our church:

> For her birthday last year, instead of asking for toys from her friends, our daughter Lucy wanted to do something for Children's Mercy Hospital—this was entirely her idea. . . . For the last year she has filled a piggy bank with any loose change or gifted money, and even would take her tooth fairy money from under her pillow and put it straight into the bank. Today we took $247.73 and had a shopping spree for art supply donations [for the hospitalized children at Children's Mercy].

Included with the note was a photo of this young girl standing by her shopping cart, arms filled with coloring and painting books. I'm looking at the image as I write these words, and she has the biggest smile on her face. Here's a picture of a kid filled with joy! I have dozens and dozens of stories like this, of children being moved to make some kind of sacrifice for others. In every case the children report feeling great joy from the experience and significantly lower desire for gifts for themselves.

The same has been true in my life. Giving actually quiets my desire for more while increasing my sense of satisfaction and happiness. It really is "more blessed to give than to receive."

Love

The last antidote to craving or inordinate desire is simply love. As we saw earlier, Jesus spoke of the two great loves—love for God and love for one's neighbor—as being central to "all the Law and the Prophets" (Matthew 22:40). These two loves are woven throughout the Ten Commandments, and they come very much into play as we fight the temptation to covet.

Love, as Jesus describes it, is not a feeling but a way of living, acting, and being. It happens when we seek the good of the other. When we bless, encourage, care for, and build up the other. We cannot love our parents and dishonor them. We cannot love our neighbor and kill them. We cannot love our neighbor and sleep with their spouse. We cannot love our neighbor and steal from them. We cannot love our neighbor and falsely accuse, gossip about, or slander them. And we cannot love our neighbor while fostering a craving for what is theirs and plotting to take it from them.

Each morning I wake up, slip to my knees, and thank God for the new day and for the blessings of my life. I pray for my family and for others on my prayer list. Then I offer my life to Christ, inviting him to transform and deliver me and to give me the strength to follow him. I ask him to help me love him with all my heart, soul, mind, and strength, and to love my neighbor as I love myself. When I'm focused on this mission, I've found that my desire for the things others have, or things I shouldn't have, is dramatically weakened. This mission reminds me daily that life is not all about me.

When you meet someone whose life and mission are focused on loving and serving others, it's hard not to be inspired. These people exude contentment and find joy in their lives. That, I think, is what God was trying to point us toward in this commandment.

I was on my way home from Egypt, where I'd been filming small-group videos for book clubs and classes studying this book. As I entered the plane, I was greeted by a friendly flight attendant named Roberta Alpert. She was exuberant. As I looked at her name tag, I noticed she was the plane's purser—the chief flight attendant, responsible for the care of all the passengers and the other staff.

Before takeoff, Roberta welcomed me and all the other passengers. As she walked by my seat, we struck up a conversation. She told me that she'd been a flight attendant for *fifty-eight years.* She began flying three years before I was born, starting on the propeller-driven DC-3. Of Delta's 25,000 flight attendants, she was number three in seniority. (She would have been number one based on her time in the industry, but she flew for TWA and others before settling in with Delta). She could have retired with generous benefits years earlier, but she told me she didn't want to stop. Now in her seventies, she was still flying full-time.

I visited with Roberta several times throughout the flight. Each time, I was struck by her boundless energy and kindness. She and her crew were always going above and beyond to bless the passengers. They would bring extra snacks, offer extra desserts, or check to see if anyone needed an extra blanket. They clearly wanted to make the experience something special. When I asked Roberta to tell me about what drove her, she pulled out a piece of paper with a talk she shared with her flight attendants before the passengers step on board:

> My personal manifesto: STOP, THINK and LOCATE every bit of kindness, compassion and gentle consideration for every living breathing being on this aircraft. . . . Think—magnanimous—dare to be vulnerable, as though it were our very first flight! Surprise someone with a complimentary something—anything. Go 1 step above and beyond what they ask for. Somehow find a way to say YES!!! It's not possible to reach everyone, but if I ask you to be "extraordinary" I will have to follow suit. I find that spirit to be contagious. . . . There are still some passengers who have waited (and saved) their whole life just to be on our flight today.

She noted that some people look at her when they get on the plane and wonder what this older woman is doing still serving as a flight attendant. But once you saw her in action, you knew why Delta placed her in charge of the flight attendants on their international flights. She was truly exceptional. She told me, "Once, a man got on the plane and said to me, 'I prefer Air France to Delta.'" She replied, "I love Air France too, but Delta has one thing they don't have." "What is that?" the man asked. "They don't have me, and I've been here fifty-eight years, and I *love* my passengers, and I live to give them the best care I can give them." This was her mission. She told me, "I love what I do."

What keeps Roberta Alpert young—what motivates her and fills her with joy—isn't having more. Her deepest desire is to serve others, to love and bless them. When I asked her if I could share her story, she smiled and replied, "I'm Jewish, and I am going to be in your book?" "Yes," I told her. "You exemplify contentment, gratitude, generosity, and love." I think she learned these qualities from her Jewish faith, shaped by the Ten Commandments.

One other thing Roberta told me. Before each flight begins, she hands out small bags of confetti to her flight crew and tells them to "throw kindness around like confetti!" At Christmas last year I received a package in the mail from her that included a photo of her in front of her first plane, the old DC-3, and a couple of bags of confetti, reminding me, too, to throw kindness around like confetti!

Coveting is a hunger, a craving to have more, a narcissistic approach to life focused on self-fulfillment that is ultimately insatiable. But being grateful, generous, and kind leads to contentment, satisfaction, and joy.

Which is I think what Saint Paul was getting at when he wrote, "Owe no one anything, except to love one another; for the one who loves another has fulfilled the law. The commandments, 'You shall not commit adultery; You shall not murder; You shall not steal; You shall not covet'; and any other commandment, are summed up in this word, 'Love your neighbor as yourself.' Love does no wrong to a neigh-

bor; therefore, love is the fulfilling of the law" (Romans 13:8– ✝
10, NRSV).

We've explored the meaning of each of these Ten Words that God spoke to the Israelites. We've learned about their historical context, and we've seen how Jesus read them, looking to the deeper meaning of each commandment (the "thou shalt" behind each "thou shalt not"). I've tried to help you see how each command speaks to us today.

As this book comes to a close, I want to encourage you to memorize the commandments. Use them as an outline for prayer, inviting God to help you to be the kind of person reflected in their words. Post them somewhere where you can see them and regularly reflect upon them, allowing them to shape your heart and life.

That leads me to a final word about a remarkable woman I love: Sonia Warshawski. Despite her diminutive stature, no taller than four foot nine, she is known as "Big Sonia" to thousands of people who have met her—if not in person, then through the feature-length documentary about her by the same name.

I met Sonia seven years ago at her tailor shop only a few miles from the Church of the Resurrection. Her shop was located in the basement of a shopping mall, the last tenant in a building about to be demolished. Sonia had run this little shop for thirty-three years in that location. The space was no more than eight hundred square feet, the walls lined with hundreds of spools of thread. Old commercial sewing machines filled up the space on one side of the shop. At the back of the store, hundreds of altered garments hung on rods, waiting to be picked up.

Sonia was eighty-eight when I met her, still working full-time. In fact, she continues to work; having relocated her shop to a new location when the mall was torn down, she's running her tailoring shop at age ninety-five. It isn't the money that keeps her working but the people and her drive to serve. When we sat down together, I asked her to tell me her story. She started by rolling up her shirtsleeve to reveal the numbers on her forearm: 48689. Sonia recounted how as a teenage girl in Poland, she was "sniffed out" by the German shepherds as she hid under the floor beneath her bed. Her father and brother were shot by the Nazis. Her little sister escaped, and Sonia was taken to Majdanek concentration camp with her mother. There they were separated by an SS officer. Her mother was sent to the gas chambers, and Sonia would be sent to Auschwitz-Birkenau. She spent the next two years there before being transferred to Bergen-Belsen. When the British arrived to liberate the camp in 1945, she was struck by a stray bullet yet survived.

In our conversation, I asked Sonia about forgiveness, a question she'd clearly been asked on many occasions. She told me, "I don't have the authority to forgive what was done to others. But I *will not hate*." Then I asked her about the large sign below the counter that greeted customers as they entered the shop. You simply couldn't miss it.

The sign? It was the Ten Commandments. Sonia had put it on prominent display not to proselytize or persuade but as a statement of the principles or rules that shaped her life. Sonia explained that philosophy like this: "We were meant to spread love. We are to put goodness in our hearts. And we were made to help others where they need help." Then she added, "That's what keeps me going."

The Ten Commandments were not only the first thing

that customers saw when they entered Sonia's shop but also the first thing she saw as she opened the doors every day. They were a reminder of who she was and how she hoped to live her life. And despite the horrible trauma she'd experienced as a young woman, these words still struck her as the essence of what it means to be human. If anything, the Holocaust reinforced the importance of these commands to her.

In the end, the commandments can shape you and me just as powerfully. They were given to us by a loving God who longs for us to experience what Paul calls "the life that really is life." They were intended to be not onerous burdens but guardrails and guideposts that protect us and point us to the life God intends. My hope in writing this book is that you might find, as Sonia did, that these commandments are, in fact, words of life.

What You *Might Say to Jesus*

At the end of each chapter, I've offered a few words that I sensed Jesus might say to you in light of the commandment we'd just read. But as we close this book, I'd like to invite you to offer these words to him:

Thank you, O Lord, for the gift of these Ten Commandments. Jesus, help me to live them as you interpreted them. Forgive me for the many ways I've violated them. Help me to trust in you, to walk with you, and to love you. And help me to love my neighbor as I love myself. May these words be for me guardrails and guideposts. May my heart and life be shaped by you and defined by these sacred words of life.

· · ·

You may want to photocopy or even cut out this page and tape it where you can see the commandments each day, reciting them, reflecting upon them, and praying them as you seek to live them.

THE TEN COMMANDMENTS

I am the LORD your God, who brought you out of the land of Egypt, out of the house of slavery;

    I. You shall have no other gods before me.

    II. You shall not make for yourself an idol.

    III. You shall not make wrongful use of the name of the LORD your God.

    IV. Remember the sabbath day and keep it holy.

    V. Honor your father and your mother.

    VI. You shall not murder.

    VII. You shall not commit adultery.

    VIII. You shall not steal.

    IX. You shall not bear false witness against your neighbor.

    X. You shall not covet.

Acknowledgments

I am deeply grateful for my editor at Convergent Books, Derek Reed, whose editorial skills and probing questions made this a much better book. Thank you, Derek! Thanks, too, to Campbell Wharton, Tina Constable, and the entire team at Penguin Random House who made this book possible. I also want to thank the amazing copy editor who worked on catching my errors and correcting my grammar! Thank you Hilary Roberts!

I'm grateful for my agent and friend, Roger Freet, whose encouragement and input in developing the concept for this book was invaluable.

Thank you to Susan Salley and Alan Vermilye and the team at Abingdon for your partnership in developing small group leader guides, videos, and children and youth components so that entire congregations can study *Words of Life* together!

I'm grateful for James Ridgeway and the team at Educational Opportunities who provided travel, accommodations, and guides for the time I spent in Egypt, retracing the life of

Moses and the historical backdrop to the Ten Commandments. The videos that accompany this book were filmed largely in Egypt. This would not have been possible without Educational Opportunities.

Thanks, too, to Julian Zugazagoitia, and the Nelson-Atkins Museum of Art, for allowing us to film portions of each video study in the gallery as they were hosting the *Queen Nefertari: Eternal Egypt* exhibit. Nefertari was the beloved wife of Pharaoh Ramesses II. If a late date is assumed for Moses, Nefertari was Egypt's queen as Moses led the children of Israel out of Egypt. Having items from her time period, including her sarcophagus, in Kansas City as we filmed was a treat.

Special thanks to Sandy Thailing who traveled with me to Egypt to film the small group videos and then who edited and produced them.

My gratitude to the people of the Church of the Resurrection. I love this congregation, and the ideas that made it into this book were first shared with them in sermons over the last thirty years.

Finally, I want to acknowledge my wife, LaVon, who has been my constant companion, closest friend, and muse for nearly forty years. As a full-time pastor, I write after hours—evenings, late nights, on my day off, and on vacation. LaVon gave up hundreds of hours we might have spent together in order to allow me to write this book. Her feedback and input as I was writing was invaluable. And she has sought to live these commandments with me over the last four decades. I love you dearly, LaVon.

Notes

INTRODUCTION

1. Richard Dawkins, "Why I Want All Our Children to Read the King James Bible," *Guardian,* May 19, 2012.

2. Adam Hamilton, *Making Sense of the Bible* (San Francisco: Harper-One, 2014).

The First Tablet: The Call to Love God

I. AT THE CENTER OF IT ALL

1. This history is fascinating and clearly overlaps with the biblical story in Genesis and the opening chapters of Exodus. Also of interest, many of the pharaohs of this period had "Moses" or the variant "Meses" as a part of their names. In Egyptian the name means "son of," and it usually had the name of an Egyptian god as its prefix. Rameses, for instance, was son of the god Ra.

2. We'll consider in great detail the significance of this name when we come to the third commandment, so here I'll offer only an over-view.

3. Throughout the book I'll refer to what Christians call the Old Testament as the Hebrew Bible, recognizing that for my Jewish friends the Old Testament is not "old" but their Bible.

4. This is a hotly contested topic. Some believe Moses lived in the fifteenth century B.C., while others date him to the fourteenth through the midthirteenth century B.C.

5. The roles of the various gods, and the understanding of which was preeminent, changed over the long history of Egypt's ancient religion. But for much of that history, Amun-Ra was the Zeus of Egypt's pantheon.

6. From "Hymns to Amen Ra," translated by Francis Llewellyn Griffith, published in 1917 in *The Library of the World's Greatest Literature,* which can be read at https://www.bartleby.com/library/poem/1848.html.

7. See, for example, Leviticus 18:21, 2 Kings 23:10, and Jeremiah 32:35.

8. Sam Huenergardt, CEO of AdventHealth's Mid-America Region.

II. THE IDOLS WE KEEP

1. Akhenaten, Egypt's king from 1353 to 1336 B.C. (pharaoh during Moses's early adulthood, if we assume a late dating for the Exodus), offers an interesting exception to this rule—he sought to reform Egypt's religious life, teaching what appears to have been an early form of monotheism, the worship of the Aten—the sun—and while he de-emphasized the old gods, he did not completely forbid their worship. Many have wondered what connection there might have been between Akhenaten, who was, after his death, considered a heretic, and Moses, who launched the great monotheistic religions.

2. Often the Egyptians' temples would house multiple gods as well.

3. The chronology of the events at Mount Sinai can be confusing when reading Exodus. Most mainline scholars believe this is because Exodus (as well as the rest of the Torah) is composed of a variety of sources that were brought together to create these books, leaving inconsistencies in chronology. On the one hand, it appears Moses remained on the mountaintop for forty days after receiving the commandments. On the other, there seem to be multiple times when Moses has come down and gone back up the mountain.

III. "I SWEAR TO GOD!"

1. If you're looking for the real Adam Hamilton, you can follow me at https://www.facebook.com/PastorAdamHamilton/.

2. *The Jewish Study Bible* uses the Jewish Publication Society translation of the Tanakh.

IV. REDISCOVERING THE JOY OF SABBATH

1. Ben Wigert and Sangeeta Agrawal, "Employee Burnout, Part 1: The 5 Main Causes," Gallup Workplace, July 12, 2018, https://www.gallup.com/workplace/237059/employee-burnout-part-main-causes.aspx.

2. Brené Brown, "3 Ways to Recharge When You're Burned Out," Oprah.com, n.d., http://www.oprah.com/inspiration/brene-brown-how-to-handle-burnout#ixzz5zKm2UVGD.

3. Johns Hopkins Medicine, "Study Suggests Medical Errors Now Third Leading Cause of Death in the U.S.," news release, May 3, 2016, https://www.hopkinsmedicine.org/news/media/releases/study_suggests_medical_errors_now_third_leading_cause_of_death_in_the_us.

4. Daniel S. Tawfik et al., "Physician Burnout, Well-being, and Work Unit Safety Grades in Relationship to Reported Medical Errors," *Mayo Clinic Proceedings* 93, no. 11 (November 2018): 1571–80, https://www.mayoclinicproceedings.org/article/S0025-6196(18)30372-0/fulltext.

5. See Professor Cox's article by the same name: Harvey Cox, "The Market as God," *Atlantic,* March 1999.

6. Mark Buchanan, *The Rest of God: Restoring Your Soul by Restoring Sabbath* (Nashville: Thomas Nelson, 2008), p. 60.

The Second Tablet: The Call to Love One's Neighbor

V. A QUESTION OF HONOR

1. See Marten Stoll and S. P. Vleeming, eds., *The Care for the Elderly in the Ancient Near East* (Leiden, Netherlands: Brill Academic, 1998).

2. Administration for Children & Families, "Child Abuse, Neglect Data Released," news release, January 28, 2019, https://www.acf.hhs.gov/media/press/2019/child-abuse-neglect-data-released.

3. See Exodus 21:17 and Deuteronomy 21:18–21. Verse 20 of the latter passage implies that there is more to this violation than simply not listening to, or rebelling against, parents. These verses also raise their own moral questions related to putting one's children to death.

4. I am not aware of Chapman applying his work on the love languages to adult children and their parents, though he may have. Most of his material relates to marriage, parents raising children, and the workplace, but the quizzes on his website and his books

and resources are easy to translate to the relationships between adult children and their parents. His website is https://www.5love languages.com.

5. For a history of Social Security, see Social Security Administration, "Historical Background and Development of Social Security," n.d., https://www.ssa.gov/history/briefhistory3.html.

6. Barbara A. Friedberg, "Are We in a Baby Boomer Retirement Crisis?" Investopedia, April 29, 2020, https://www.investopedia.com /articles/personal-finance/032216/are-we-baby-boomer-retirement -crisis.asp.

7. The Gospels mention other siblings of Jesus, but both Catholic and many Protestant traditions see these as cousins or children of Joseph's by a previous marriage. Even Methodism's founder, John Wesley, seems to have believed this. Hence it is easy to understand why Mary's ongoing care was so important to Jesus as he hung on the cross.

8. Judith Graham, "Without Safety Net of Kids or Spouse, 'Elder Orphans' Need Fearless Fallback Plan," Kaiser Health News, October 4, 2018, https://khn.org/news/without-safety-net-of-kids-or -spouse-elder-orphans-need-fearless-fallback-plan/.

VI. THE TRAGEDY OF VIOLENCE, THE BEAUTY OF MERCY

1. For a discussion of these last three topics, I would refer the reader to two books I've written, *Confronting the Controversies* (Nashville: Abingdon, 2005) and *Seeing Gray in a World of Black and White* (Nashville: Abingdon, 2010).

2. Jeff Asher, "The U.S. Murder Rate Is Up but Still Far Below Its 1980 Peak," FiveThirtyEight, September 25, 2017, https://five thirtyeight.com/features/the-u-s-murder-rate-is-up-but-still-far -below-its-1980-peak/.

3. Michael Harriot, "Why We Never Talk About Black-on-Black Crime: An Answer to White America's Most Pressing Question," The Root, October 3, 2017, https://www.theroot.com/why-we -never-talk-about-black-on-black-crime-an-answer-1819092337.

4. Erika Harrell et al., "Household Poverty and Nonfatal Violent Victimization, 2008–2012," Bureau of Justice Statistics, November 18, 2014, https://www.bjs.gov/index.cfm?ty=pbdetail&iid=5137.

5. Alex Yablon, "Internet Gun Sales and Background Checks, Explained," The Trace, January 7, 2016, http://www.thetrace.org /2016/01/internet-gun-sales-background-checks/.

6.   The Forgiveness Project, "Victoria Ruvolo," n.d., https://www
     .theforgivenessproject.com/stories/victoria-ruvolo/.

VII. FAITHFULNESS IN AN AGE OF PORN

1.   Ancient Egyptian texts have been found accusing various persons of
     sleeping with other men's wives. We also know that nearly every
     ancient law code included a law prohibiting a man from sleeping
     with another man's wife and prohibiting a married woman from
     sleeping with another man.

2.   Sleeping with an unmarried woman was, however, seen to violate
     that woman's father's rights, reducing her value as a prospective wife
     and thus reducing the bride price that a father might receive for her,
     or the father's ability to find a husband for her. For this reason, Deu-
     teronomy 22:28–29 required payment to the woman's father if a
     man slept with an unmarried woman. Yet this was not considered
     adultery, even if the man was married.

3.   Walter Wangerin, *As for Me and My House: Crafting Your Marriage to
     Last* (Nashville: Thomas Nelson, 1987), p. 196 and following.

4.   Aleksandr Solzhenitsyn, *The Gulag Archipelago,* Part 1 (New York:
     Harper & Row, 1974), p. 168.

5.   Robert Scheer, "The Playboy Interview with Jimmy Carter," *Play-
     boy,* November 1, 1976.

6.   The one caveat with the GSS data, it seems to me, is that it comes
     from face-to-face interviews, which I think would make it harder
     for those being surveyed to admit to having had an affair.

7.   Paul J. Wright et al., "Personal Pornography Viewing and Sexual
     Satisfaction: A Quadratic Analysis," *Journal of Sex & Marital Therapy*
     44, no. 3 (April 3, 2018): 308–15.

8.   Samuel L. Perry and Cyrus Schleifer, "Till Porn Do Us Part? A
     Longitudinal Examination of Pornography Use and Divorce," *Jour-
     nal of Sex Research* 55, no. 3 (2018): 284–96.

9.   Aleksandra Diana Dwulit and Piotr Rzymski, "Prevalence, Patterns
     and Self-Perceived Effects of Pornography Consumption in Polish
     University Students: A Cross-Sectional Study," *International Journal of
     Environmental Research and Public Health* 16, no. 10 (May 2019):
     1861.

10. Joe Madden, "Porn Addiction Could Ruin Your Sex Life and
     Here's Why," *Cosmopolitan* (UK), September 30, 2016.

11. Michael H. Keller and Gabriel J. X. Dance, "The Internet Is Over-
     run with Images of Child Sexual Abuse. What Went Wrong?" *New
     York Times,* September 28, 2019.

VIII. WE'RE ALL THIEVES. YES, EVEN YOU.

1. Mary Ellen Biery, "Restaurants' Margins Are Fatter, but Competition Is Fierce," *Forbes,* January 26, 2018.

IX. STICKS, STONES, AND THE POWER OF WORDS

1. This quote is from a draft of a manuscript Darryl Burton has prepared for publication.

2. To find out more about Darryl Burton and the organization he heads, Miracle of Innocence, visit his website, www.miracleof innocence.org, and watch for his upcoming book.

3. Michael Barthel, Any Mitchell, and Jesse Holcomb, "Many Americans Believe Fake News Is Sowing Confusion," Pew Research Center, December 15, 2016, https://www.journalism.org/2016/12/15 /many-americans-believe-fake-news-is-sowing-confusion/.

4. Among the more popular are FactCheck.org, politifact.org, Snopes .com, RealClearPolitics.com, and TruthorFiction.com, though by the time you read this there may be others.

5. Monica Anderson, "A Majority of Teens Have Experienced Some Form of Cyberbullying," Pew Research Center, September 27, 2018, https://www.pewinternet.org/2018/09/27/a-majority-of -teens-have-experienced-some-form-of-cyberbullying/.

6. Not her real name.

X. KEEPING UP WITH THE JONESES

1. Lauren Sher, "Couple Celebrates 80th Wedding Anniversary, Shares Secrets to Lasting Marriage," ABC News, November 20, 2012, https://abcnews.go.com/US/john-ann-betar-celebrate-80th-wedding -anniversary-share/story?id=17769043.

2. Purchased prior to 2005 but taking into account stock splits in 2005 and 2014.

3. Kimberly Amadeo, "Average U.S. Credit Card Debt Statistics," The Balance, May 1, 2020, https://www.thebalance.com/average-credit -card-debt-u-s-statistics-3305919.

4. Warren Clarke, "What's the Average Car Loan Length?" Credit Karma, December 9, 2019, https://www.creditkarma.com/auto/i /car-loan-term/.

5. Saint Augustine, *The Confessions,* book 1, chapter 1.

6. Adam Hamilton, *The Walk: Five Essential Practices of the Christian Life* (Nashville: Abingdon, 2019), chapter 1.

7. Hamilton, *The Walk,* p. 24.

ABOUT THE AUTHOR

Adam Hamilton is the author of thirty-one books on scripture, practical theology, and the Christian life that have, together, sold more than three million copies. He is the founding pastor of the United Methodist Church of the Resurrection in the Kansas City area. The church began with four people in 1990 and today numbers more than 25,000 regular attenders. His passion in both writing and preaching is to bring together excellent scholarship and practical pastoral application so that readers and hearers might grow deeper in their faith. Adam earned his undergraduate degree in pastoral ministry from Oral Roberts University and his master of divinity degree from Perkins School of Theology, Southern Methodist University. He has been married to LaVon for thirty-eight years, and together they have two daughters and one granddaughter.

Facebook.com/PastorAdamHamilton
Twitter: @RevAdamHamilton
Instagram: @revadamhamilton

I n this six-week study based on his book *Words of Life,* Adam Hamilton brings modern eyes to the most important set of ethics in history. For churchwide Lenten study or for small groups any time, readers will consider the commandments in their historical context, consider the meaning of each commandment in Hebrew, unpack how Jesus reinterpreted them, and show how every "thou shalt not" was intended to point to a life-giving "thou shalt."

In addition to the Leader Guide, which includes session plans, activities and discussion questions, a youth leader guide, a children's leader guide, and a DVD are available. The DVD features Adam Hamilton teaching on-site in Egypt and insightful conversations with Rabbi Art Nemitoff.